The Last Voyage of the Loch Ryan

The Last Voyage of the Loch Ryan

ANDREW STRUTHERS

author of THE GREEN SHADOW,
CHOMOLONGMA, *& etc.*

NEW STAR BOOKS
Vancouver
2004

New Star Books Ltd.
107 – 3477 Commercial Street
Vancouver, BC   V5N 4E8
www.NewStarBooks.com

Publication of this work is made possible by grants from the Canada Council, the British Columbia Arts Council, and the Department of Canadian Heritage Book Publishing Industry Development Program.

Printed and bound in Canada
First printing, August 2004

LIBRARY AND ARCHIVES CANADA CATALOGUING IN PUBLICATION

Struthers, Andrew, 1961 –

   The last voyage of the Loch Ryan / Andrew Struthers.

ISBN 1-55420-008-3
   1. Struthers, Andrew, 1961 – .   2. Tofino (B.C.) — Biography.
1. Title.
FC3849.T63S78 2004   971.1'2   C2004-903768-4

The Last Voyage of the Loch Ryan

They that go down to the sea in ships, that do business in great waters; These see the works of the LORD, and his wonders in the deep. They mount up to the heaven, they go down again to the depths: their soul is melted because of trouble.
They reel to and fro, and stagger like a drunken man, and are at their wits' end.

PSALMS 107:23-27

Prologue

I SAT UP LATE THAT NIGHT IN THE WHEELHOUSE of my fish boat, long after the rest of town had gone to sleep. I had a serious decision to make.

But my mind kept drifting. There was something hypnotic about the pool of light that lay on the chart table. The warm breeze blowing steadily through the porthole smelled of low tide and piling tar. The smell of home. The red eye on the shortwave radio blinked, and a tiny voice flitted into the wheelhouse like a blackfly: "Auntie, are you on this one?"

It was a little girl over in Opitsaht, the Native village across the channel from Tofino, which some local wag had dubbed "Opposite".

Silence.

The radio's eye winked again, and her auntie came on: "Yes."

Now how did Auntie know she was the right auntie? That's the mystery of a small town. Each human life is invisibly connected, like roots tangled in the duff beneath the ancient rainforest, a forest so vast and thronged with creatures that humans find themselves busted down from tyrant to citizen. But don't let insignificance bother you. Out here, even the constellations get lost among the lesser stars. Preconceptions break down and rust in the back of your mind. Redskin, redneck — those are just words. What is real are these ghost voices on the radio, a little girl finds her mother's sister in the ether, while water slap-slap-slaps against my hull

silence

the smell of cedar. The scent of diesel. In the morning, white sheets of mist lie tangled between giant trees, and some old guy standing on the dock says, "It'll burn off by noon." Which it never does. Stunted spruce combed sideways by the sea wind. A yellow eye-stab of lichen on gray rock. Welcome to Clayoquot Sound. Fifteen years in the arms of this goddess, and tonight is my last.

The Plan: Leave Tofino before dawn. Ride five miles out on the falling sea. Catch the tide as it floods back into Juan de Fuca Strait. Make Victoria by midnight. Drop anchor across from the Legislature. Read a list of demands through a bullhorn. They're going to be sorry. You can kick a man out of the Clayoquot, but you can't kick the Clayoquot out of a man.

The Problem: Tomorrow's journey will take me through that godforsaken stretch of kelp and rock marked on older charts as the Graveyard of the Pacific.

I used to think the nickname "Graveyard" was a little unfair. A bad roll of the dice, like gunpowder. You take three harmless substances (sulphur, saltpetre, charcoal), mix them just right and — bam! — your skull's an ashtray on some Chinese history professor's desk. Same with the Graveyard, except the three ingredients are geography, geology and history. Geography, because the currents of the North Pacific drive any vessel that loses steerage en route from San Francisco north onto the shore between Sooke and Tofino. Geology, because that shore comprises miles of giant stone teeth, sheer cliffs and shifting sandbars. And history, because in 1897 gold fever hit the Yukon, and soon every decrepit tub on the west coast was pressed into service carrying the hopeful north, right into the mouth of the Graveyard. Old-timers in Tofino tell some pretty grim tales about what happened next.

The Norwegian freighter *Tatjana* lost its rudder in a summer storm and got skewered on a pinnacle near Tatoosh. Waves the size of steam trains smashed into the hull. Launching the lifeboats was impossible. But the captain glimpsed a column of rock rising from the spume, halfway to shore. A stepping stone. They tied a rope to a seaman's ankle, dangled him over the side and swung him like a yo-yo until they got him past the breaking waves. He bodysurfed to the base of the column, where he was alternately sucked away from the sheer rock and dashed back against it. Barnacles tore off his nails and shredded the meat on his palms as he scrabbled up the face. At the top he found a little fir tree growing in a crack. His hands were now such ragged claws it took him twenty minutes to tie the rope around it. When he finally got the rope fastened he tugged it, and a cheer came across the dark waves. The crew strung a hawser to the rock and a second to the shore, and an hour later they had swung along it to safety. All were saved.

Of course, most vessels didn't have that kind of fortitude to fall back on. The aging *Hera* creaked out of Seattle with only a box of dried peaches, a few sacks of coffee and a supply of salt horse that was deemed by her two hundred passengers to be of inferior quality. She went down right in front of Tofino harbour with 750 barrels of beer, a shipment of lime and a prefab church in her belly.

For sheer tragedy it's hard to top the demise of the steam ship *Valencia,* hung up on a rock pile near Pachena Point less than sixty yards from shore. She keeled over until the deck was awash, and 117 men and women swarmed up the rigging, which now lay horizontal across the waves. Other vessels stood off for days, watching as, one by one, the ship's company succumbed to exhaustion and dropped into the sea like ripe plums.

But for sheer comedy the *Clara Nevada* gets the nod. She set out from Seattle with the second mate already in the brig for drinking. The chief steward was such a brigand that the captain had to physically restrain the crew from throwing him overboard near Bamfield. The engineer was a complete incompetent. He only got the job because he was a Mason. They rammed the cutter *Grant* while backing out of Yesler harbour. They shattered their bowsprit against the wharf at Port Townsend. The terrified passengers signed a petition begging the Port Townsend harbour master to seize the vessel, but he had no authority to do so. She went down with all souls off Lynn Canal when a cache of contraband blasting powder hidden in the hold exploded. Years later the lighthouse keeper at Elder Rock was stretching his legs in the dawn after a great storm and found the *Clara Nevada* driven high onto the reef, with the luckless company's bones still tangled in the hoary kelp. A bona fide ghost ship.

On second thought, I decided the nickname "Graveyard" was perfectly fair. It fit like a body cast. And that's where I was headed at dawn.

The wheelhouse had grown chilly. I shut the porthole. I thought, It's two in the morning. I better get some sleep. But I couldn't sleep until I got this damned GPS figured out. It was still in "startup mode", whatever that meant. It had been in "startup mode" for hours. Perhaps there was something wrong with the battery. Piece of crap. Two hundred bucks at the Tofino Co-op and I'm supposed to trust my life to it?

"Finding satellite."

"Finding satellite."

"Finding satellite."

I wanted to smash it against the wall. I began to panic. Skipper of the *Loch Ryan?* Who was I trying to kid? I thought, This tub's a floating coffin. I know nothing of the sea. I'm way out of my depth.

I wanted to call the whole thing off, but it wasn't that simple. A few months earlier my ex-wife, Gwen, and my daughter, Pasheabel, had moved to Victoria. Which meant *I* was moving to Victoria. If I didn't get the *Loch Ryan* through the Graveyard, I'd lose everything I'd won in Clayoquot Sound. My freebooting lifestyle. My resourceful attitude. My habit of sleeping when I was tired, getting up when I was rested, checking the colour of the sky and planning the day from there. I'd have to get a regular apartment and a regular job to pay the regular bills. I'd be forced like sausage meat into some shag carpet hellhole, wage-slaving for the Man.

Shag carpeting or death. I had to choose. Outside, black water and indifferent stars stretched away forever. I rolled my options around in my head until they tangled in a knot. I thought about the first time I went salmon fishing and pulled in two lines of trolling gear at once, and it all ended up on the deck in a great fuzzy ball of hooks and cables that my skipper called an "afro". Now my whole life felt like that.

How did I end up with an afro? Just three years earlier I had been happily landlubbing it up in the grandfather forest, with no inkling of the adventures that lay ahead on the high seas.

ONE

SOME ARE BORN TO ADVENTURE, SOME FIND adventure, and some are dragged ass-backward through adventure, screaming for mercy to gods they no longer believe in. I'm in the last group. Still, it's better than a day job.

After university I tried living "on the Grid", with a day job and a credit history and a NOTICE OF DISCONNEC-TION and a stress-related skin disease, but it just wasn't me. So I moved into the forest in Clayoquot Sound and built a pyramid out of cedar and glass, perched on a hundred-foot cliff, looking out through a canopy of giant trees over a sparkling limb of the Pacific.

On the horizon lay an island where the ancient village of Echachist once stood, until it was destroyed in battle two centuries back. For years there was no sign of human activity down there. Then one evening the setting sun caught on two golden cedar beams. Someone was raising a house frame.

I asked around at the Common Loaf Bakery. The builder was Joe Martin, whose forebear had been the chief at Echachist. I watched Joe's house go up, and just before he finished the roof the Federal Government slapped a demolition order on my door. My house wasn't up to code. I moved into town for the winter, and by spring the fuss had died down, so I carried my stuff back up the hill and continued my contraband lifestyle.

To pay the bills I worked on fish boats in summer and at the fish plant in winter. My one attempt at a career was writing, but it didn't work out. I loved the writing but hated the career. These days you can't simply write, you also have to be a celebrity, which I find unsettling, because the only celebrity I resemble is Shrek.

But I gave it my best shot, and right away things got out of hand. I wrote one story — *The Green Shadow* — and next thing I knew I was nominated for a national humour award, up against Mordecai Richler. The awards banquet was at the Excelsior Hotel in Toronto. The entrée was pork — not my favourite at the best of times, and with Mordecai on one side and Paul Quarrington on the other, vying for quips, I was so nervous I couldn't eat a bite. Mordecai was just the opposite. The guy had an intense love of pork, I guess. He ate his meal, and then he ate mine. Then he wandered around the banquet hall scoring pork rinds from the plates of strangers, all the while puffing on a rancid Gauloise and swigging haughtily from a giant bottle of Cherry Jack. When the MC announced the winner, Mordecai didn't even listen. He ran, snuffling and wheezing and wiping the grease from his stubby sausage fingers on the frills of his cheap rental tuxedo, to the stage, where he grabbed the award, shouldered the MC aside and began grunting platitudes into the microphone.

Okay, that never happened. I didn't even go to the awards banquet. My account is what we fishermen call a yarn. It starts with the truth and casts off from there. What makes Clayoquot Sound's yarns unique is that the truth is often stranger than fishing. Here's what really happened that night.

The awards were the same day as the fun fair at Pasheabel's school. She had just turned six, and what she wanted more than anything in the world was to win a cake in the cakewalk. We bought a ticket and tried and lost. Bought another ticket, lost again. Third time I said, "This is all the money I have left. If we go in the cakewalk again, we can't afford to go in the haunted house."

But Pasheabel knew what she wanted. Cake. Not so much to have cake as to win cake. So round we went again, and when the music stopped we were standing on the sweet spot. Sally Mole came running up to us. "You won!"

It seemed like a good omen, and it was. I thought about Mordecai and the awards banquet. They must be announcing the winner right about now. Suddenly I knew I had won that too. It was one of those moments when it seemed the mysterious thread that sews together the lives in a small town runs deeper than anyone imagines, connecting every human life, even mine and Mordecai's.

Sally handed us an evil-looking chocolate bundt baked by Ian Bruce's kid, who was barely older than Pasheabel — but to us it was a magic cake. We took it down to Barry Grumbach's house. Barry was a crab fisherman who lived on the inlet. The night was full of stars, the inlet was flat as glass, and on the grass behind the house the usual suspects were roasting a giant ling cod and playing tunes. Halfway through the evening, Charles Campbell called from the *Georgia Straight*. "You won!"

The party went ballistic, everyone chanting, "Nice try, Mordecai!" I forget what happened next. At dawn Pasheabel and I woke up on the couch to find our magic cake had been eaten by drunks. There was nothing left except a swirly pattern on the plate where someone had licked it clean.

It seemed like a bad omen, and it was. After that night my writing career took a sinister turn. When the book version of *The Green Shadow* came out, my publisher, Rolf Maurer, a German intellectual with a huge forehead and a soul patch, sent me on a tour to flog it. The interviewers asked the same questions over and over and over until I started making the answers up out of sheer boredom, and then they nailed me on the facts. It was like spending a week downtown in a miniskirt that didn't quite cover my ass.

The low point came on CBC's *Almanac,* with Cecilia Walters. The studio was cavernous and empty. It seemed too grand for radio. It was more like a TV studio that had gone blind. I sat in the green room listening with horror as the guest before me told a harrowing tale of surviving breast cancer. When I got to the hot seat, Gloria was sobbing like a schoolgirl. This was going to be a tough act to follow.

I read a chapter, and Gloria chuckled with glee and asked if I still lived in my pyramid in the woods. Dead air. The Feds still had that demolition order on my house. If I told the truth, town council would be obliged to evict me all over again. "No," I said, "I live in a double-wide trailer on Chestermans Beach."

Back in Tough City I climbed the trail to my pyramid and found three Commercial Drive hippie chicks and an Australian shaman camped out on my floor. They had braved the pass, bushwhacked through the rainforest to my place, unrolled their bed mats, lit my oil lamps, and used my only saucer as an ashtray. They comprised what Rolf called my "fan base". I said, "You people have to go." But the Aussie had other ideas. He wanted to unblock my root chakra by laying his didjeridoo across my ass and blowing. I said, "Mister, I don't even know you."

By now you're thinking, This has got to be another yarn. Sadly, that's exactly what happened. Out here, yarn and truth get tangled. A lot of Clayoquot tales are true at one end and tall at the other. But I swear on the grave of Jesus, every tale I'm about to tell you is true at one end.

SEEN FROM DAY TO DAY, THE COURSE OF A human life remains hidden, so what looks like a backwater sometimes leads down to the Amazon. On one such eddy of a late summer evening I ran into Adam Busker, a huge guy with a missing front tooth who lived in a cabin out on Frank Island. He could only get home at low tide, and this had tied him to the cycle of the moon. He worked in construction and was a steady sort, but because the moon was the heart of his life rather than the sun, he kept odd hours. When we met up that evening it was almost dark, but he was heading down to Long Beach to surf. I chatted knowledgeably about surfing, although I'd only tried it once. He said once was not enough. I said I'd only had the chance once. He said he had an extra suit and board. Checkmate.

We pulled into the parking lot at Long Beach, that magic spot where only driftwood separates the cars from the waves. Adam cracked a green Rubbermaid tote and out slopped a soaking wad of neoprene. It was my suit. It took me five minutes to wrestle my foot into the clammy leg. Finally I said, "Is it meant to be so tight? I can't bend my knee."

Adam said, "That's because you've got your leg down the sleeve."

Once my legs and arms were in the right places we carried our boards down to the waves. Adam lay on his board and paddle-wheeled his arms. I did the same. The first wave looked pretty small, around three feet. Suddenly it reared up, knocked me off my board and tumbled me like a sock in a spin cycle. The next wave did the same. And the next. Twenty waves later there was a lull. I paddled like mad and made it over the lip of the next wave just before it crashed. The roar sucked away like a fleeing crowd, and it got so quiet I could hear gulls. The sun lay on the horizon behind three surfers, who were standing right up on the water like some magic Jesus hat-trick in the Rembrandt light. Foam champed at the glassy slope behind Adam. He had caught a good one.

Then the ocean gathered up in front of me with a low rumble. I cowered behind my board. It was a mistake. The wave drove the board into my face so hard my fillings rang like xylophone keys, then tore it from my hands. A fingernail bent back, soft and sickening. My ankle got yanked down by the leash, all the way down, and it got very loud and very cold. I saw the boiling underbelly of the wave pass overhead, water seemed to rush in at me from all directions, then I shot out the back of the wave with an enormous gasp. I couldn't catch my breath. My nose and chin where the board hit were numb as holes. I dragged myself ashore and puked and watched the others surf. This was not the sport for me. But it was too late. I had seen that holy rolling moment surfers call the Break, and it drew me back, like heroin stroking the thigh of a horny poet.

A week later I met Al Anderson at the coffee shop. Al and I had been friends since we met at community college in Prince George, years before. In those days he was a real straight arrow, and I was twisted like a balloon animal. He had a job and a bank loan, and I didn't even have a bank account. One night we went to the ATM. When the screen asked Al how much he wanted to deposit, I typed in $30,000 as a joke. The machine spat out an envelope. Al, caught up in the spirit of the moment, licked it and stuffed it. His balance shot up to thirty grand and change. "I'm rich!" he said.

We laughed and laughed.

Next time he went to the bank the manager took him aside. "We're not going to press charges," she said, "because we don't think you knew what you were doing." All weekend he'd had a $30,000 limit on his Visa. We could have bought a jeep and hightailed it to Mexico. Years of loan payments were wiped away in a single night of hanging out with me.

Now, a dozen Septembers later, we sat at the coffee shop in Tough City and watched the tourists leave in chevrons. The surf place next door was selling off its battle-weary rental suits for a hundred bucks a pop. I still ached like I'd been shot out of a cannon, but I waxed lyrical about my surfing adventure. Al asked how often I surfed. I said if I owned one of those suits I'd be surfing right now. Al said he could lend me a hundred bucks. Checkmate.

Once I'd spent the hundred bucks I felt obliged to go out. After a month my shoulders hurt so much I went to the doctor. He said, "It's called getting in shape." That spring a terrible hurricane hit Tahiti. On Al's TV we watched grainy footage of tin-roofed huts coming apart in a hundred-mile wind. Poor devils. But their national tragedy was our double overhead. A day later the swell hit Long Beach, and for the next week I only came ashore to eat and sleep.

What kind of freak spends the day zipped into a tight rubber suit with a leash, getting whacked on the ass and shins with a giant board until he feels like a neoprene piñata? A surfing freak. Yet despite my devotion, I sucked. I didn't beat sections, I didn't hang ten. If I managed a bottom turn it was a miracle. But I didn't care. There are two kinds of great surfers: those who catch great rides, and those who have great fun. In the latter category I was world-class.

Even on the shortest day of the year I found myself running down the beach, listening to ice crystals crunching under the sand. Out at the Break, hail pinged off my board. The water was cold as a banker's handshake. Waves drummed slowly against the black rocks, and in the fog around me a murder of surfers cowled over their boards like strange offshore birds, arms crossed for warmth, glancing at each other.

A set rolled in, booming, a big sound torn from the bottom of the ocean. Whoops came across the water. Heads went down. Boards hove towards the rocks like shearwaters' wings. I heard the avalanche roar behind me, then I was grabbed like a stick and hurled at the rocks. I popped up. The blinding hail was sweet after the brine. I forget what happened next. I rode over the back of the wave before it carried me inside the Break and sat down again. What the hell just happened? Every time I caught a ride like that I blanked out. I only remembered the moment afterward. While I was up, my mind was reduced to a single flash, like the tip of a lathe cutting into right now.

It began to snow. I watched the flakes vanish on the surface of the sea. The rhythm was hypnotic. I felt like that snow, like I was dissolving into the landscape.

That winter I surfed so much that when I closed my eyes I saw a distant horizon with sets of waves rolling endlessly towards me, and I seemed to rise up and down on them. There was a constant warm glow in my belly, as if the freezing water had set my thermostat up a notch. At night I lay by the woodstove and read books by the Swiss philosopher Carl Jung, and by day I surfed or hung out with Pasheabel. Life was perfect.

Jung wrote about thirty books, mostly on the human soul. Somewhere in all those words he suggested that perfection was overrated because it excluded wholeness, which by its nature must include imperfection. I knew what he meant.

My life felt perfect, but there was still something missing. I was thirty-five, so naturally I assumed that what I was missing was a lover. Two years earlier I had fallen madly in love with a young hippie woman called River, but she left town to go traveling, and now she was married with children, in Ireland. After her came a stream of lovely young hippie women, but every one of them reminded me of River, like a photocopy of a photocopy of a photocopy, until I could make out the grainy pattern of an empty love life.

Then an artist waif called Shelby drove up from the city in a green VW van, and she was not like the others. She loved junk food, art and the criminal mind. To pay for cigarettes and gas she waitressed at the Schooner, a big old building that had been barged down from the airport after the War and was now a restaurant.

The owner, Maré, loved to have fun. She ran the Schooner on a need-to-party basis. She hired Shelby and me to put on a murder-mystery dinner theatre. It was such a hit that she asked us to do something else. We came up with a "Rites of Spring" bacchanal. For the poster I did a drawing of Shelby riding a skateboard, naked. Maré loved it so much she put it in a hundred-dollar frame and hung it on the Schooner wall. I had already told Shelby I was going to give her the drawing, but I didn't have the nerve to tell Maré I needed it back.

One day Shelby and I walked past the Schooner and saw the drawing through the window. She said it should be hers. That night I thought, She loves art and she loves crime. I bet she'd really love art crime. Art is about breaking the rules. Rules are what make up the law. Therefore, breaking the law can be a form of art.

I planned every detail. At dawn I would go down to the Schooner, sit at the table right under the drawing and order breakfast. The waiter leaves. I slip the drawing into my pack. I make some excuse and pop next door to the Co-op, which has the only colour photocopier in town. Dismantle the frame. Photocopy the original. Mount the copy in the frame. Slip back into the Schooner. Put the framed forgery back on the wall. Walk out the front door with the original in my pack, cool as what the French call *un concombre*.

Next morning I slept in. By the time I reached the Schooner it was the middle of the breakfast rush. Instead of a faceless waiter, my friend Anne appeared with a notepad. I was so flustered I ordered the first thing on the menu — the Amish breakfast. She left, but there were two Germans sitting right under the drawing. I tried making small talk to find out if they had already eaten, but I went too far, babbling about sea pressure and the economy until they turned from me in fear. I stood up and pretended to notice there was something wrong with the drawing. Flushing like a beet, I lifted it down and slipped it into my pack. The frame was so big that it stuck out the top by a foot. I folded my coat over it and loped out the front door.

I sat on the retaining wall in the Co-op parking lot and tried to dismantle the frame. I had imagined a couple of Swiss clips and some tape, but the frame was put together like a bank vault. As I fumbled, everyone in town walked past. "Hey, Andrew, I just read your book!" "Yo! Struthers! Gonna run for mayor again?" Finally I got the drawing out. I bolted into the Co-op and discovered there was a ten-minute lineup at the copier. When I reached the front, the phone in the office rang and the cashier handed the receiver to me. It was Anne. She said, "Your Amish breakfast is getting cold."

How the hell did she know where I was? I cursed the mysterious membrane that connects the lives in a small town. I tried to photocopy the drawing, but it was too big. I had to copy it in two parts and tape them together on my knees in the toilet of the Alleyway Cafe, sweating now from every pore.

When I got back to the Schooner the Germans were gone. I clunked the forgery into place. The two pieces had already begun to buckle along the seam. It wouldn't fool a chimp. I had to get out of there. I gobbled my Amish breakfast — eggs, sausage, bacon, cheese, a farmyard on a plate — while sweat trickled down my nose. Anne loomed over my shoulder. "Where did you take the drawing?"

I panicked, mumbled some lame excuse through half-chewed meat and ran towards the big front door. It swung open, and Maré stood there, framed by morning sky. She laughed. "A couple of Germans came upstairs and told me some bald guy just stole a drawing right off my wall. I said, 'Oh, that's just Andrew. He did that drawing. He must need it for something.'"

I laughed too, and slipped past her into the cool air. I cycled over to the organic store and gave the drawing to Shelby, who worked at the till. She said the Schooner had just called and wanted to know where their drawing was. I bit the bullet, cycled back and explained my new rule-breaking art form to Maré. She didn't buy it. Halfway through she let out a furious roar and smashed the forgery on the restaurant floor.

The weed of art crime bore bitter fruit. Shelby moved to Vancouver and got a job on a TV cop show called *Da Vinci's Inquest,* where art and crime were one, and I was left alone up at my pyramid, contemplating my misdeed. The silent summer days only made my conscience louder. The image of Maré's unhappy face tormented me. Art crime. What the hell was I thinking?

One evening Pasheabel and I watched the sun drop into the sea like a golden coin. I said, "Not a cloud on the horizon."

She asked when she'd be able to see the horizon. I pointed between the trees. "It's right there."

"You mean where the sky goes down to the sea?" She was crestfallen. For years she had thought the horizon was some magical place only grownups could see. I chuckled, but I had an uneasy feeling that I was missing something just as big.

One afternoon, while pondering what that thing might be, I wandered down to Fourth Street dock. It was a miserable day, with rain pelting the naked alders. I decided to visit Peter Schultz, who lived in an old salmon troller with his daughter Malaya. She had been born in the house next door, back when I lived on Chestermans Beach. First time I saw her she was ten minutes old, still ringing like a bell with the song of the big sky, still connected to the source by blue and red cords bright as electrical cables curling from her belly. I said to Peter, "She looks like a little Buddha."

He said, "She'll get over it."

When she was two he built a cabin in the forest below the pyramid from the kind of lumber mills call "three sides good". Snapshots of Yogananda, crystals, chainsaws, cedar chip carpeting, Fisher-Price toys and the scent of sandalwood and gasoline. When the Feds chased him out he bought an old fish boat called the *Pacific King* and converted the hold into a living room. She was moored at the end of Fourth Street dock.

The foul weather made Peter's wheelhouse seem all the more cheerful. The oil stove blasted out the BTUs, and the pragmatic voice on the weather radio chanted its bad weather mantra: "Visibility near zero, wind ten to fifteen knots, with a light south-easterly swell . . ." Through the curved front window, Meares Island rose in a wall of ancient trees. Malaya sat down in the fo'c's'le cabin with her toys jumbled around her little legs. I said, "Not bad for four grand."

"And Betty Crocker's selling that one for three," Peter said, jerking his thumb at a bedraggled tub lashed next to the *King.* It was the *Loch Ryan,* Derek Arnet's old boat. Years earlier I had almost deckhanded on her. My best friends at the time were two crazy South American refugees named Jose and William, or as Ralph Tieleman called them, Jose and Hose B. One day Jose called from Vancouver. "I'm stuck. You wanna deckhand for me on the *Loch Ryan?*" But by the time I found the boat, Hose B had taken my place, so I never fished her. Now it seemed she had fallen on hard times.

"Why so cheap?" I asked. "I thought these boats were fifty grand."

"Not since the Mifflin Plan," said Peter. "The skippers just want to get rid of them. Good deals for us."

The Mifflin Plan was a federal program designed to preserve salmon stocks by reducing the size of the fishing fleet. Between 1995 and 1997 Ottawa bought back half of the salmon licences on the west coast. It looked good on paper, but it worked out badly for wooden boats. Of the 2,000 licences retired, 1,800 had wooden hulls. Few metal and fibreglass boats were retired because they were newer and cheaper to run. The remaining fleet fished twice as hard, so not a single salmon was saved. But suddenly the bottom fell out of the market for wooden fish boats. One guy on the dock bought a boat for a dollar. A *Canadian* dollar.

The wheelhouse of the *Loch Ryan* was green with mildew, and the engine wasn't running. But I remembered her from better days. She was real cozy without the mildew. There was a neat little fo'c's'le cabin in the bow, an oil stove in the galley, and a table nook in the wheelhouse that folded down into a bed.

The owner was a little old lady called Betty Krawczyk, Raging Granny and author of *Clayoquot: The Sound of my Heart*. Betty grew up in Louisiana, where she had so many husbands and babies that to make ends meet she had to sell stories to women's magazines like *True Confessions*. During the Vietnam War she moved to Canada to keep her son Mike out of the army. She bought property up near Cypre River, and she had been going back and forth in a tin launch with a nine-horse Evinrude. One day she was almost run over by a packer coming out of the harbour, and after that she felt unsafe in her little boat.

When the Feds floated the Mifflin Plan, one of the skippers who bit was Derek Arnet. He had been trolling the *Loch Ryan* for seven years, and like most fishermen, he loved his boat. But with the licence gone she was suddenly a moorage bill. He sold her to Betty for ten grand.

The wharfinger at Fourth Street dock, Art Clarke, was a practical man. He once fixed a deep fryer with a coat hanger. The idea of a little old lady driving a fish boat around his harbour made him nervous. "Now, Betty," he said, "when you want to come in, just call me on the radio and we'll send someone out to help you dock."

But it turned out the boat stayed up at Cypre for months at a time. A leak developed, the bilge pump ran till it drained the battery, and she took water up to the engine block. Peter went out to Cypre and bailed her with a gas pump. When he checked the oil, water shot out the dipstick hole. That's not good. Rumour had it the hull was tight but the engine was hooped, and this had driven down the price. Betty had bought her for ten thousand and was asking three and a half.

"You should buy her," said Peter.

I'm no good at making big decisions like that. The bigger the decision, the more confused I get. When the decision is life-changing, I become paralyzed. This leaves the decision to its own devices, which are better than mine. First time I met Gwen, who I was to marry, the decision had already been made. First time I saw the spot where I built the pyramid, it was as if the pyramid already stood there for a moment. The back wall was black with tar paper and the stove pipe was smoking. And when I saw the *Loch Ryan* moored next to Peter's boat, the same thing happened. The rain stopped for a moment and the water around the hull went dark and glassy. The chipped white paint on the wheelhouse seemed to glow. Perhaps it was a trick of the light. Or perhaps I had seen the future, and it floated.

I stood there in a lover's daze. I had been toying lately with the idea of leaving the forest and returning to the realm of bread and circuitry, but the spectre of the Grid horrified me. Life on the *Loch Ryan* seemed like an ideal compromise. I would be attached to the Grid, but not *on* it. I could bob to one side of the North American Dream.

This is where surfing paid off big time. I had spent countless hours bobbing happily on the ocean's breast, so the idea of living on the water didn't fill me with anxiety, as it would have done two years earlier. I told Pasheabel we might be getting a new place in town. I watched her face as we walked along the shore. When we turned onto the dock she looked surprised. "We're going to live on a boat? Neat!" She squeezed my hand, and that cinched the deal.

I phoned Betty. "Oh-h-h, that boat. What was I thinking? I had this fantasy of chugging around Clayoquot Sound, typing away in little coves. But I can't keep up with the maintenance. It's like a bad marriage."

"I'll give you three grand," I said.

"I'll take it."

I put up a poster in the Bakery:

DEMOLITION PARTY
The Forces of Order Have Caught Up With Me!

That weekend I sat on the top of the pyramid and gazed into the valley below. I had gone down into it only once or twice, to cut snags for firewood. It had felt untouched, like the dawn of time. Now a line of candles wended up through it, and the whole place rang with hippie chick laughter.

I encouraged my guests to kick holes in the walls while I chainsawed through the floor boards. Windows were carried down the trail and made into cold frames. The kitchen sink was torn out, set in the middle of the floor, and used to burn the kitchen cabinets. By dawn the pyramid had been transformed. Only the four main beams remained. What had been my home for seven years was reduced to four towering triangles of rainforest and a cedar platform.

I cooked eggs and bacon over the old sink. With the walls gone I could see much more of the ocean. The sky was overcast, and the water shone like glass. I brewed up one last cup of coffee, but already I was gone from that place. Far below, the horizon peeped between the trees. That's where I was headed now.

TWO

"HEY, ART! THE LOCH RYAN SOLD!" SAID PETER.

"Finally! Well, just tell whoever bought it there's no live-aboards. We already got too many, we're getting complaints. Who bought her?"

I stuck my head out of the fish hold. "I did, Art."

"Oh. Morning, Andrew. Well, you can stay till you get her fixed up."

Art figured I was okay because I got up with the sun, a habit even deadbeats like me develop when there's no electricity. Art had the habit bad because he had been born miles off the Grid at Hot Springs Cove, where his dad owned the land the springs are on. It seemed like Art had been the wharfinger in Tough City since the world was young. He ran the dock out of a shed at the top of the ramp, where the Fishermen's Club met for breakfast at six every morning. The menu never varied: ten cups of bad coffee and a million-dollar view.

The only person who was supposed to be living on the dock was Shorty, a pint-sized Russian with pierced nipples and a cowboy hat, who ran a little knife shop out of an old fish boat moored on the second finger. Each knife was a piece of art honed from hand-forged steel with a scrimshawed bone handle. His boat was stuffed full of tools, paintings, carvings and giant bottles of Demerara rum. Art had grandfathered him into the paperwork because the Feds allowed one live-aboard per harbour, to cut down on vandalism.

But scattered between the first and fifth fingers of the dock were at least a dozen others. Next to Shorty lived old Johnny Madokoro, whose dad had taught the settlers how to troll for salmon back in the thirties. Johnny had a house up in Port Alberni and lived on his boat while he was fishing. When he was a young man he had owned property over on Stubbs Island, but he was of Japanese descent, so when the War came the Feds seized his house and tore it down. I said, "I know how you feel."

Lashed to a log off the end of the dock was a double-ender with a cabin on top. In it lived Lance, his wife, and their baby. Lance had grown up in Ontario, where his dad took to beating his mom. One day the old man started up right at the dinner table, so Lance knocked him out cold with a ketchup bottle. His mom said, "You better be gone when he wakes up." Gone he was. He made his way west until the forest came down into the sea, and now he jigged cod and drank all day.

On the fourth finger, a mandolin player called Ryan lived in a big green sailboat with no mast. He was a chef by day, and every night a ring of hippies sat on his cabin roof plucking bluegrass.

At the very end of the fifth finger, moored between Peter and the *Loch Ryan,* was a giant wooden seiner called the *Oldfield.* She was painted black from bow to stern except for the windows and looked like she could take out an icebreaker. She started life as a halibut boat up in Prince Rupert in the thirties, then became the tow-off boat for herring season in the Clayoquot. Now she was a pirate ship. The hull seemed to be formed from hundreds of coats of lumpy paint, the crew subsisted on a steady diet of gooseneck barnacles and beer, and every night there was a party on board with reggae pumping from the wheelhouse at nosebleed volumes.

The skipper was a pirate named Chris, who in summer went tuna fishing a thousand miles out, leaving the helm to his second in command, Turtle — sixty years old and four feet tall, with a bushy black beard and a shaved head. Turtle always wore a dinner jacket and a tie, and his laugh was so loud it made sheet metal vibrate. Town council passed a bylaw making it illegal for him to laugh after midnight, so he moved down to Bamfield, where a rich family gave him a donkey, and he rode around on it laughing freely. He dug clams down there until 1995, when the Feds changed the bottle deposit, after which, as local bard Crabber Dave lamented, "A clam's worth a nickel, and a can's worth a dime." Turtle returned to the Clayoquot, took a herring skiff up to Ahousaht and brought back a load of empties. For a winter he was rich, but the resource didn't last. Now he was back scraping gooseneck barnacles with Chris and the crew.

Scraping goosenecks is like a halfway house between work and rehab because you can make a bundle with just a pair of gumboots and a barnacle scraper and get right back to drinking. In 1986 I was on the very first gooseneck test fishery, with Barry Grumbach, Al Anderson and Mike "Conehead" Bickle. We left Weigh West dock in the dawn mist. Five minutes, twenty metal horses and a lungful of salt air later we dragged the boat onto an intertidal rock near Stone Island.

"These are goosenecks," said Barry, peeling up a mat of vegetation from the slippery surface beneath our feet. Strange centipedes and undersea beetles scuttled for cover. The goosenecks looked like translucent carrots torn from a monster's ass. We gawked, hungover and skeptical. What kind of fool would pay good money for something scraped off a harbour rock? I could see the Main Street sewer outlet from where I stood. But apparently if you cooked them in lots of garlic butter and stuck them on a plane to Portugal, they became a delicacy. And they covered the rocks in such a thick toupée that by the time the tide lapped at our heels, our sacks were full.

The return of the tide is the bane of the barnacle picker. A boat drops you on a rock, breaks down on the way back and it's The End. Roll credits. Young Andrew played by . . . Fade to black. Every year some luck-pusher gets washed away. But I felt pretty safe that morning because Barry ran the crew like a platoon. He held the boat's nose to the rocks, gunned the motor and pointed at each of us in turn. "In. In. Wait." Conehead was the one who had to wait. He clung to the gunnel, inches from my face, so that I was looking right into his eyes as the freezing water rose around his gonads and his face sharpened like an ice pick.

"In." Conehead splashed aboard like a big loofah and whined all the way to Long Beach dock, where the buyers were set up with scales. We made about a hundred bucks apiece. But money that comes in with the tide goes out the same way. We tied up at the pub and ate lunch, and next thing I knew it was dark, and soon we were throwing dice right at the bar with two Québecois called François and Gaston and a miniature cabinet salesman from California. Low roll bought a round of Jack Daniels. It shows you how things have changed. Today you can't even smoke in that pub.

The Yankee lost four rolls in a row. François leaned forward, picked up his shot glass with his lips and downed it. "Bet you can't do it again," said Gaston, signalling us to watch. When François lowered his lips around the next shot glass Gaston brought his palm down hard on his pal's head. The glass shattered. Gaston howled with laughter. Barry said, "You and your friend better cool it."

"He's not my friend! " said François. "He's an ass'ole! He go bap! on my 'ead! He fuck my woman . . ." They launched at each other across the table. We dragged them outside. In the foyer we ran into Conehead, who had gone to check out the Yankee's E-type Jag.

"That guy's got a Saturday night special and a roll of hundreds in his glove compartment. He wants us to take the boat down to Mexico and fill her with drugs. I'm frightened."

Gaston lay unconscious on the rubber welcome mat. From the dark parking lot we could hear the Yankee's girlfriend screaming at him. We took François down to the boat, where he sucked a giant hot-knife hit of hash from the blowtorch, leaned back, and just kept leaning back until his skull hit the deck. We dragged him up the plank and laid him beside Gaston. Barry shook my hand. "Home team, two. Visitors, zero."

I began to wonder if I really wanted to go back to university in the fall. There was too much fun to be had right here in the Clayoquot, firing guns in Barry's basement and learning to operate giant pieces of machinery. The beauty of the place was, there were no rules. You could do anything your mind could conceive. So I built a sixteen-foot scale model of the Great Pyramid in front of my house on Chestermans Beach. While I was working, the new cop puttered up on a motorbike. It seemed like there was always a new cop in town. I guess the Feds didn't want them getting too close to the locals. He said, "You're not going to live in there, are you?"

I said, "It's solid sand."

He said, "That's okay then. It's just, there's too many people camped on the beach. We're getting complaints."

Within weeks my solid pyramid was overshadowed by a virtual one when Barry's girlfriend, Crystal, showed me a crumpled photocopy. It was a list of names and a letter that said she could make $10,000 in a month, with no money down. All she had to do was mail $50 to the name at the top of the list and give $50 to her mom for recruiting her. Then she could sell two "shares" to friends at $50 a pop, and they'd tell two friends, and so on, and so on . . . like that old shampoo commercial.

It looked good on paper. A hundred bucks goes out, a hundred bucks comes back in, and a month later ten grand would show up in the mailbox as Crystal's name rose to the top of two hundred lists. But she knew there was something fishy about the deal. I showed her the math. It would take more friends than yet existed upon the Earth to finish building the Pyramid. Barry, ever practical, said, "So let's change the list and put Crystal's name at the top."

But to do that she'd have to stiff her own mom. If we went up a level to include her mom, we'd have to stiff her mom's best friend, and so on, and so on . . . The architects of the Pyramid were wise indeed.

Around then the menfolk went clam digging up at Mosquito Cove, and when we got back, Pyramid fever had spread through the better half of town like a distaff infection. Everyone was doing it, until Julie from the pub recruited the new cop's wife, and the next day everyone got busted. When the Pyramid of Women collapsed lovers fought, friendships foundered, homes were wrecked. It was like all ten plagues of Egypt in one. That cinched it for me. What a town. Even the women were up to no good. I decided to stay.

A decade later, Fourth Street dock seemed like a last enclave of the brand of anarchy that made Tough City great. But it never fails — when you find paradise, there's already trouble brewing. The tension revolved around the first finger, which was crowded with aluminum boats of the kind called "beer cans". They were skippered by Chinese fishermen who lived over on the mainland and only came to town to crab. A lot of old-timers had never forgiven the Chinese for ruining the clam fishery. Jack MacDonald said to me, "Before that crew showed up there was so many clams you could dig 'em with a backhoe. Now there's none left."

I had seen that crew at work one winter, weighing clams on the big red scale outside Art's shed while the buyers waited in cube vans. Six of them went at it like a troop of Beijing acrobats, throwing sacks onto the scale and grabbing them off so fast that it took me a while to realize only five sacks were being moved. The sixth sack got weighed and paid for fifty times.

But stunts like that don't impact a fishery like a backhoe does. I was pretty sure old Jack's misgivings were based on an irrational fear of the colour yellow. I knew how he felt. Like a lot of people, I had been afraid of the Chinese ever since I read that if they all jumped up and down at the same time, the seismic shock would create a tsunami that would take out the west coast. Read it in *Ripley's Believe It Or Not*. Believed.

Later I grew up, but many still believed. Just change "jump up and down" to "work for nothing" and "seismic shock" to "labour surplus", and you have this year's model. It didn't help race relations on the dock that summer when suddenly the coast seemed crowded with rusting hulks, packed with desperate human cargo and run by Chinese gangsters. And I'm not talking about BC Ferries.

The human cargo came mostly from Fujian, China's last great forest. Beijing calls it the "green treasury", which has an ominous yet familiar ring. Fujian also ranks first in hydro power production because of the swift rivers that tumble down through the Wuyi Mountains to the coast, which is a major source of seafood. It's mostly rural, although industry is spreading up the coast from Hong Kong, and the economy is going off like a string of firecrackers, growing an average of thirteen percent per year. Except for the part about the booming economy, it sounds just like BC. So why were these folks risking their lives to come here?

It's a tradition that dates back to the Opium Wars of 1840, when Britain forced the Qing dynasty to sign treaties supplying cheap labour to the west. In the 1880s, 9,000 "coolies" built the railroad through the Rockies, mostly recruited from Fujian. These men loved working on the railroad because it gave them a chance to journey in search of the Fortunate Land, a place of limitless opportunity from childhood fables. The railroad companies loved them because they did work no one else would do — laundry, cooking, women's work — for half the going wage. Exactly half. That was the law. But once the railroads were finished and the regular women showed up, the coolies became a liability. On July 1, 1923, Chinese nationals officially became *personae non gratae*. Happy Canada Day. Until 1947 the True North remained strong and free of Chinese, the only flavour ever banned from the Canuck melting pot. But the Fujian dream of finding the Fortunate Land never died.

In 1991, the life of the Chinese peasant took a serious downward turn when the government started paying farmers for their crops with IOUs. On top of this, every year four million peasants were forced off their ancestral lands to make room for conveyor belts carrying stuffed toys, and ten million students left school to enter the labour market. It was a human tsunami.

To enjoy the peasant life a worker had to rake in eighty-five cents an hour. But down in the new factories, Mr. Gap could only afford to pay eighteen cents. The alternative was to cut a deal with the Snakeheads. For $40,000 this smiling, shark-eyed crew could whisk you away from a life of drudgery to an entry-level position in the North American garment industry.

I'm an immigrant myself. I came from Scotland, the nation that built this country. First prime minister: Macdonald. Longest river: Mackenzie. Top inventor: Alexander Graham Bell. It sounds like roll call at my Glasgow grade school. But getting kicked off your farm by the Man, flushed down to the coast, turned away from overcrowded factories, and ending up as boat bilge is also a Scottish tradition.

The tradition dates back to the eighteenth century, when Glasgow sat on a mile-deep seam of coal. Up sprang the largest shipyard in the world. Scottish engineers became such a cliché that their frantic accents echoed down through the decades and into the future: "The engines canna take it, Captain!" North of Glasgow stretched forests aplenty and rivers teeming with so many salmon that it was illegal to feed them to the hired help more than three times a week. Yet Scots were showing up in Canada in such droves that the Mc's and Mac's have their own section in the phone book.

The exodus was sparked back in 1742 when the English Parliament passed the Highland Act. Among the menaces proscribed were Gaelic and bagpipes. Now, bagpipes I can understand — but as a result of the language barrier, the Scottish gentry became Anglophiles. First they were educated in England, then they moved to England, then they developed English accents, and eventually they hated Highlanders worse than the English did.

The foundation of the English economy was wool. To this day the Chancellor of the Exchequer, who balances the books, sits on a symbolic sack of wool in Parliament. The displaced Scottish nobles knew their ancestral home would make ideal sheep-grazing land, but it was full of Highlanders subsisting on tiny farms called crofts. So they sent the tenants packing and replaced them with cheviot sheep, which local wags renamed "four-footed clansmen". It was the beginning of what the landowners craftily dubbed the Highland Improvements, later known as the Clearances.

Over the next century, tens of thousands of two-footed clansmen were chased down to the city, where the new factories could not absorb them, and so they ended up on boats bound for Canada, such as the *Sarah*. She had been transporting slaves to the Americas until new humanitarian laws forbade her to carry more than 489 slaves per trip. But the Scots were a free people. Such laws didn't apply to them. When the *Sarah* left harbour in 1801 there were almost seven hundred porridge-eaters crammed into her hold. Fifty of them died en route.

Hundreds of vessels were pressed into service to exploit this legal loophole. Dozens vanished without trace. One in five immigrants succumbed to typhus, cholera and the terrible smell of damp wool. Between 1815 and 1838 more than 22,000 displaced Highlanders arrived in Nova Scotia. In 1841, Quebec complained that it was unable to provide welfare to the legion of destitute Scottish refugees.

Scotland eventually learned to love the sheep. They've even begun to clone the best-looking ones. But the Highland economy never recovered. I grew up in the Highlands, whiling away countless summer hours in the harbour at Stonehaven, damming up the river that ran alongside the pier until the harbour master chased me. The pier was made from massive red sandstone blocks with ancient rusted metal rings set in them. When the tide dropped the boats would sit on the sand, tilted against the stone pier. At midday I hid from the sun in the cool V of shade under my favourite boat, a wooden-hulled beauty by the name of *Aberdeen Rover.*

One evening there was a crowd of people around the *Rover.* I heard a lot of fast chatter. The crowd dispersed and someone shook the skipper's hand. He wore a strange expression, which I later realized was despair. Next day *Aberdeen Rover* was gone, another victim of the economic malaise that lingered in the Highlands for centuries after the Improvements.

When I was twelve my parents said we were leaving Scotland in search of greener pastures, or at least ones with less coal slag. They had scrimped and saved for twenty years and still couldn't afford a house. I wasn't sure what scrimping was, but it sounded degrading and I wanted out. We had been reading *Beautiful British Columbia* magazine, sent every month by my Aunt Babs from Vancouver, along with reports of unbelievably low prices for peaches and cars. To us, BC was the Fortunate Land. It was nearly impossible to get in, but dad was willing to do work no Canadian would do — teach high school in Prince George.

His wage tripled overnight. We bought a house the second month. Shortly after we arrived my mum collapsed with gallstones. She'd been in terrible pain, but kept quiet in case we were turned away at the border. That's the kind of stunt people pull to reach the Fortunate Land.

Later, four girls in a car parked outside Woolco howled with laughter when they saw me coming. "Hey, kid, you're ugly! Do you know that?" I saw my reflection in a car window: fake leather jacket, red floodpants and a flowery green shirt, topped off with mirror shades I bought at the Drug Mart so I'd look like the sheriff in *Cool Hand Luke*. "My God," I thought, "I'm an immigrant kid."

It hurt, but not like a beating from a Snakehead. In any case, reaching the Fortunate Land was worth the pain. The beer-can crew along the first finger of the Fourth Street dock knew that. They made the most of everything. In the evenings the men came back from crabbing and their wives cooked seafood in smoking woks right on the floats. The scent of hot oil and rising diphthongs carried across the water like music. I knew they kept soft-shelled crabs. I knew they weighed their clams twice. But I also knew too much to wish them gone. Fourth Street dock was a small world, and any trouble that came to them would come to all of us. Of course, when trouble did come, it wasn't what any of us had expected.

THREE

"STILL ASLEEP, HIPPIE?" IT WAS A GLORIOUS spring morning, and suddenly there came a loud rapping on my wheelhouse door. I staggered out on deck. Ralph Tieleman stood on the dock in his gray Stanfield's sweater. Tough City was a town full of outsiders, but only Ralph had elevated alienation to an art form. No one knows how Ralph got so unique. My theory is he grew up at Happy Harry's gas station playing with engine blocks instead of the kind that have letters on them.

The first time we met was downstairs at the Maquinna Hotel, among the forest of red terrycloth tabletops that could soak up a round of beer and still keep your cigarettes dry. Two strippers twirled on the semicircular stage. The older one was tall and lithe and danced like a gymnast, but she had cracked thirty, so the drunks were cruel. She gave as good as she got. She swung provocatively round the brass pole, fired a withering line into the table at the front, arched over backward, zinged the crew by the jukebox, and so on. It was quite a routine. I was impressed, but not turned on.

The younger woman sported blond ringlets and breasts like six-guns that Ralph called "'toons". She was eighteen, but she looked twelve. She said she was just starting out. In fact, this was her very first time. She tried to swing around the pole and fell on her ringlets. The drunks cheered her on. She pointed at the front row from the stage. "You guys are all a bunch of sweethearts."

But earlier in the day Conehead told me that those two had dunked their car in the ditch at Brown Rice Corner. He got them back on the road and they invited him home to Room 222, where their clothes were piled on a waterbed the size of Kennedy Lake. They ordered champagne in a bucket and it came out that the youngster had been dancing for years. The virgin story was just her shtick.

When the dancing virgin finished her routine, Ralph bought her a beer and she sat at our table wearing a blue silk kimono that was open down the front. I was so nervous I couldn't find anywhere not to look. Everyone congratulated her on her debut.

"But I made so many mistakes!" she said.

"Then I guess I'll have to spank you," said Ralph, who wasn't buying anything except the beer.

Years later I slipped coming down the trail from the pyramid and stepped on Pasheabel's foot. Ralph drove past in his monster truck and saw her crying. He picked us up and took us to his house for hot chocolate. His place was amazing. There were three half-built Harleys in the living room, surf boards stacked against the wall, junk piled on every surface. He showed me a mechanically de-boned chicken in a can. The thing was still in one piece. He called it "trailer park food". He showed Pasheabel a toy tugboat he had made for his ex-girlfriend's kid. It was the best toy I'd ever seen. It even had a boom of tiny logs he'd sawn from pencil-sized branches.

When I told him I was looking for work, he hired me to paint the pub with him. After that we painted the fire hall. Around then the Feds stapled their demolition order to my pyramid door. I ran for mayor, hoping to save my house, but I lost by five votes. Ralph got us a gig painting the council chambers. "Cheer up, Struthers," he said. "You can't fight City Hall. But you can paint it a different colour."

We were proud that we didn't depend on tourists for a living. Don't get me wrong. One on one, I never met a tourist I didn't like. But as a group they're the plague of the twenty-first century. In a good summer, Tough City had a thousand locals and a million tourists. That's a thousand to one against. It was the questions that disturbed me most. They asked why the bank was only open three days a week. They asked if the sandbar in the harbour was an iceberg. One woman asked Mary MacLeod where the tide went.

Ralph and I did nothing to remedy their confusion. On our lunch break we would sit behind a table of tourists and talk loudly about "sport logging" or the new craze of paint-ball whaling, and how difficult it was to get the protective goggles onto the whale. But there was no turning back the human tide. Every year, town had more tourists and less community spirit. There wasn't even a community centre any more. The old community centre on Main Street, built back in 1917 with foot-thick beams and a shake roof, had suffered a cruel twist of fate.

In 1972 the Feds kicked all the hippies off Long Beach to make way for the park, and a few of them spruced up the old community centre and called it the Gust of Wind. But because the newcomers subsisted on beans and rice, some local wag changed Gust to Burst. By the late seventies the joint was jumping. Maureen Fraser sold cheese buns and coffee through a flap near the front door. On weekends they showed movies in the room upstairs. There were carving tools and cedar chips everywhere, and a pungent smell of pot. Finally town's old guard got together and shut the place down. Maureen started a hippie bakery called the Common Loaf, which quickly became the Common Loafer, and the Burst of Wind became the town library.

The librarian was Linda White, daughter-in-law of old Bill White. In those days I lived on Chestermans Beach with my wife's folks, Moira and John. Bill would stroll down the beach and shout up at the window to see if John was about. Then they walked for miles along the sand, two old guys with white hats, while Bill told stories about Tofino back in the twenties, when the only contact with the outside world was the steam launch *Princess Maquinna,* once a week down at the Whiskey Dock.

From these half-heard tales I formed my first impression of town before the road came through. Something about how everyone kept cows for milk, and one morning all the cows were standing on the Whiskey Dock, and when the *Maquinna* pulled in there was a bull on board. Something about the coroner, who would bellow, "I'll do the coronizing around here!" when anyone else tried to guess the cause of death. Something about the blaster, who one afternoon sent a two-by-four through Bill's front window, then slipped in, measured the frame and left without a word. The next week a new window arrived on the *Maquinna.*

Back then no one had locks on their doors, but these days the closest town got to common ground was the checkout at the library. When Pasheabel quit school halfway through Grade 3, I relied heavily on the library to home-school her. By home-school, I mean I showed her how to work the microfiche, then got out of the way while her mind went off like a bottle rocket. She ordered books by the cartload about whatever caught her fancy. First it was dogs, then monkeys, then donkeys, then pilgrim times. I begged her to stop reading and go outside to play, but she was insatiable. She spent so much time among the stacks that it was like a second home, except with electricity.

As the winters passed, the library's shake roof began to leak, and by the spring I bought the *Loch Ryan,* Linda had to set out buckets among the books. An old wooden building is like an old wooden boat — if you keep up with the maintenance it lasts forever. But there might be a grant from the Feds if we built a new library from scratch. Rumour had it that Pasheabel's second home was going to be torn down. Town's memories would end up homeless, but no one seemed to care. It was raining tourist dollars in the Sound right then, and we were all too busy setting out buckets.

It was tourist dollars that had brought Ralph down to my boat that spring morning. I made some coffee and we stood on the deck, staring up at the perfect blue sky. But for Ralph, perfect wasn't good enough. He shook his head uneasily. "Looks like there's a system moving in."

I said, "What system? The solar system?"

"There's a job up at Quait Bay," he said.

That could mean only one thing. We were going to paint the Floatel.

Once this coast was thick with Douglas-firs three hundred feet tall. Independent loggers called gyppos felled them by the dozen and boomed them down to Vancouver, where they were milled into beams called BC toothpicks. Each toothpick was sixty feet long and three feet by three feet. Nine filled a flatbed train. Most of the toothpicks were shipped back east and sawn into two-by-fours for the Ontario housing market, but somebody once used a couple of flatbeds' worth to construct a gigantic barge. A sawmill and two houses were built on top, then it was floated up the coast and used to log remote inlets.

Fifty years later the forests were gone. The barge was

moored in False Creek for Expo '86, the houses and sawmill were torn down and a three-storey hotel was built in their place. After the fireworks, a sports-fishing outfit bought the floating hotel and shipped it from False Creek up to Barkley Sound. The hotel floated, but the sports-fishing outfit sank without a trace. A millionaire stockbroker bought the monstrosity and barged it up to Quait Bay, just round the point from Raging Betty's property at Cypre River. His plan was to create a wilderness retreat for the mega-rich. But first it needed a new coat of paint.

I got in Ralph's monster truck and we drove to the old BC Packers dock, where we met Randy, a big guy with a Tom Selleck moustache and two storeys of speedboat. He said the job was huge, but he wanted to keep it in town if he could. We rode up to Quait Bay on the top floor of his launch. The Floatel was moored at the back of the cove with giant chains anchored in the mud.

"Holy crap," said Ralph as we pulled up at a float the size of Fourth Street dock that had been tacked onto the side of the thing. "Acropolis Now."

When the first Europeans showed up, the Natives called them *mamaalthi,* which means "floating house". They had never seen anything as big as a schooner float before. Now I knew how they must have felt. I realized right then that tourist money was going to win out, and town would soon be butchered for parts and changed into something strange and new, just as Chief Wickaninnish must have known when he saw those towering blankets the *mamaalthi* called sails.

Randy led us through ballroom after ballroom until Ralph became distraught. He didn't want this gig to interfere with his surfing schedule. These days he lived to blow the local teenage surf crew's mind, a grouchy old cyclops on a ten-foot Onionhead, with water dripping from his ZZ Top beard. He said, "I think I'm going to pass."

Then he said that I should paint the place myself. That way I could pay off the boat and get back to my bill-free status. Randy liked the idea. He figured I could run the crew and supplies back and forth on the *Loch Ryan*. I said the engine wasn't running. He said he would set up a tab for me at Whitey's fuel dock.

Whitey Bernard was a west coast fixture. When he was six the War began, and he watched from the crowd as the troops marched down the hill to the docks in New Westminster. When he saw his dad go by, he ran after him and grabbed his hand. A photographer caught the moment and it ended up on the War Bonds. When the fighting was over, BC Hydro sent Whitey to Clayoquot to hook Tough City up to the electrical grid. He married, had kids and eventually became mayor. Some folks found him abrasive, but I figured it took chutzpah to set up a fuel dock in the heart of Nuu-chah-nulth territory and call it Whitey's.

The place had everything: engine parts, boat tools, copper paint for the hull, fibreglass, even heavy-gauge machine chain from the days of chain-drive steering. Randy's offer was like getting a tab in Aladdin's cave of wonders. I said I'd do it, and we shook.

There was only one small problem. I was mechanically declined. I once changed the oil in my rusted Datsun and it never ran again. If I so much as glanced inside a machine, a sweat came over me and I lost all reason. My father-in-law, John, had the same problem. When he came down to London to fight in the War, the army tested his mechanical aptitude by getting him to assemble a bicycle. He got the lowest mark in the platoon, so they put him on the bomb squad. It sounds crazy, but it worked. A lot of sappers died simply because they were guys, and after a month they figured they'd got the hang of the whole bomb thing and stopped checking the manual. The brass knew John would never try that.

Even examining the *Loch Ryan*'s two-way radio seemed like tinkering with a bomb to me. It was a small black box, cradled over the captain's seat, that showed no signs of life. I had to get it going. A radio was essential for weather reports or to call for help if the engine died or in case there was a tsunami warning, in which case we were supposed to take our boats out to sea and ride over the swell before it jacked up and smashed the docks into matchwood. A tsunami warning sounds like a yarn, but I've seen it happen.

It was the summer of 1986. Al Anderson and I lived in a cabin on Chestermans Beach. One Sunday afternoon we got a case of beer and wandered out to Frank Island. When we got back, Laser Dave was waiting on the deck.

We called him Laser Dave because he spent his evenings lining up candles on the beach to show you where the planets would rise. He knew everything about the sky and the sea. He told us there was a three-foot swell headed this way. It had started a thousand miles out in the Pacific and was due to hit Tofino at 9:17 PM. "It should wash right up the beach and knock the logs around," he said.

It sounded exciting. Our cabin stuck out of the salal, almost over top of the driftwood logs. We were front-row centre. I put my chair out on the deck and opened a beer. Ten minutes later Gwen showed up, breathless. "Did you hear?"

"Yeah, yeah, Laser told us, three feet, nine o'clock."

"Three feet? No, it's three *metres*. We have to go to Radar Hill."

Radar Hill is the only high ground near Tofino that you can drive to. We call it Radar Hill because during the Cold War the Feds built a top-secret facility there that was obsolete before it was completed, so the village bought the building for a dollar and shipped it down to the lot beside the Schooner, where it became the fire hall. All that's left on the hill are the old cement footings. In case of a tsunami we're all supposed to get up there ASAP. But that was for a full-on tsunami. A three-metre swell wasn't going to kill anyone. I wanted to stay right where I was and watch the logs wash around.

A siren whooped outside. The new cop walked in through the lot and shouted up to us that there was a tsunami coming, it was five metres high and the beach was being evacuated. This was serious. I opened another beer and watched Al and Gwen race around the cabin, arguing about what to take, shouting, grabbing blankets, apples, a pack of cards. I still couldn't believe there was a real tsunami coming. I went outside and gazed up at the clear blue sky. The sea was flat as a newly made bed, rumpled white along the shore. It was quiet.

Too quiet.

The air grew heavy with portent. The sun cast Bible beams across the sand, and in my mind's eye I saw the waters suck back like in *The Ten Commandments*. "Where's the cat?" yelled Gwen. We couldn't find her anywhere. Finally Al tore up all the bedding and there she was, cowering in terror. He grabbed the wretched animal and threw her inside his yellow Beetle, and she hid under the passenger seat and wouldn't come out. We raced back to the cabin to get Al's sewing machine and Gwen's manuscript and the rest of the beer, thinking, It's true! It's true! And the animals know beforehand!

Turn off the gas. Grab a block of cheese. A hat. A book I'd never finish. Diver Dave came tearing up the beach on a motorbike and yelled that the wave was only an hour away.

"It's thirty-five feet high! It's thirty-five feet high!" Then he yelled something I didn't catch, about an earthquake in the Bering Sea. I'd heard about some giant volcano up there. And hadn't some scientist or psychic predicted a major earthquake? It all added up.

The top of Radar Hill teemed with locals, and a lot of them had brought beer. Sulo Hovi alone had two flats in the trunk of his shiny black car. It was Psychedelic Sunday on Rock 101. Acid blared from car stereos, and a hippie kid in a green army jacket goose-stepped past with a boombox on his shoulder tuned to the weather station. That usually calm, pragmatic voice stammered like Porky Pig. "Th-th-there has been an earthquake off the coast of Alaska . . ." The details were drowned in wail and chatter. Three-point-seven? Eight-point-seven? Something-point-seven. I yelled to Gwen, "There was an eight-point-seven earthquake in Alaska!" Her eyes went round. With her tousled hair she looked like Little Orphan Annie.

"Fifty feet!" said Al. "Fifty feet!"

We gathered on the steep south face of the hill, staring into the setting sun, row upon row of anxious faces, like a grad photo from the school of hard knocks. Our houses, our gardens, our record collections . . . all gone. The wave had reached biblical proportions and could no longer be measured in feet or metres. Beside me, Kathy Lapeyrouse wept because she'd forgotten the baby photos. Next to her a tourist said, "I heard the warning on the radio, I passed the cops, I musta been doing seventy!" He was having the time of his life because he had nothing to lose. Behind him, a beer-toting local said the Port Alberni tsunami of '65 knocked houses on their sides, put a car in a tree, caused a million dollars' damage. "Ten million," said his pal. "And it was '64."

Then a murmur passed through the crowd. "How big? How fast? When? Did you hear? It's only twenty feet high." Someone else said fifteen. Four people crouched around a radio.

"SHHH!"

The wave had just hit the Charlottes and was only five metres high. No, wait — five feet. Soon it was back to the original three. A truck gunned its diesel. The new cop told us the warning was still in effect, but no one was listening. The acid rock swallowed the weather radio, and party hearty got the upper hand. Gwen decided to stay. Al and I got in the Beetle. The cat was still wedged under the seat. Dumb animal.

Back in Tough City the bar was deserted and the TV still showed the emergency information screen. We took the last of the beer over to Barry's house, where he and Crystal had watched the whole thing on TV. In the years that followed there were two more warnings, and I ignored them both. But I wanted to have the choice, so I opened the back of the *Loch Ryan*'s radio and peered inside.

An hour later, clammy with sweat, I realized all it needed was a new fuse. I bought one at Whitey's and immediately the little black box sputtered to life and began speaking in tongues. There were a hundred channels, which seemed excessive, but I soon found my way around the dial. Channel 82 was reserved for lighthouse keepers, 21 was the weather station, 16 was for emergencies, and 68 was where the Nuu-chah-nulth hung out. All the rest were up for grabs, and you could talk to people for miles around: fishermen muttering in code about the day's catch, hippies in isolated beach cabins, Native couples shouting at each other ("I wish you were here so I could hit you!") and the occasional logging truck bouncing a signal off low cloud from up behind Kennedy Lake.

Much encouraged, I turned to the *Loch Ryan*'s three-ton diesel engine. There was an ancient owner's manual in the nook beside the compass. Exploded diagrams revealed every bolt and gasket, beautifully rendered in shades of gray. On the front was my engine's name: Allison. I hauled up the floor of the wheelhouse and there she was, her name stenciled across the rocker cover. I thought, "I'll treat her like a lady."

But Allison was no lady. She hunkered down and refused to work, like some bad-ass redneck bitch from *Jerry Springer*. She bit the skin off my knuckles. She hung me upside down till my eyes felt like bursting egg yolks. She ducked my head in the oily bilge until I looked like a balding Buckwheat. I unseized the brushes in the starter and replaced all the fuel filters and gaskets. I dismantled the blower. I figured out the fuel pump. But still she wouldn't turn over.

It looked like there were air bubbles in the fuel line. I had a nagging suspicion it had something to do with the very first fuel filter I'd replaced, but that filter shell lay deep in the belly of the boat, a dark region filled with sharp edges and wires that reeked of burnt peanuts, bilge, and diesel. I didn't want to go back down there. Finally I dangled upside down into the engine room like a trapeze artist and unbolted the filter shell. I discovered I had pinched the gasket the first time I screwed the lid back on. That tiny rubber pucker was the cause of all my grief.

When I twisted the key, how she roared! I lay on the dock feeling the throaty rumble through my back and looked up at the midnight sky. I thought, Hah! Some folks would pay a mechanic to do that.

The night was quiet, except for Allison. I was exhausted. This was why I froze like a jackrabbit in high beams every time I saw a machine. So many parts. Each of the parts was simple in itself, but every part had to work or nothing worked at all. I had always been afraid to look at the world in terms of its parts, in case I lost track of the big picture and disaster ensued. But now that Allison was in my life, I had no choice. I'd have to keep one eye on the whole and one on the parts, even if it drove me mad.

NOW THAT I WAS MOBILE AND CONNECTED, all I needed to pull off the Floatel gig was a crew. Usually I worked alone, even when I worked with Ralph. But this job was too big for one man. I scribbled a HELP WANTED ad for the board at the Common Loafer, and on my way there I stopped at the bank. Standing next to me in line was the local vegan goddess, Jada-Lee Watson, wearing an embroidered medieval blouse and listening to Megadeath on headphones. She was my pal Tom Messer's girlfriend. They had hooked up the year before when I took them both skydiving. Now they were going to have a baby, for which I felt vaguely responsible.

I told her about the Floatel, and she told me she needed a job. I asked about her work experience. Her resume was bizarre. She had been raised on a hundred-foot yacht and had sailed everywhere from the Caribbean to Alaska. Her chores included collecting flying fish from the deck every morning. Her dad had the sails rigged with rings of lignum vitae, and she would climb them like rungs to the lookout at the top of the mainmast. Some nights they were caught in great offshore storms, and this had fostered in her a deep need to execute each of her chores to the last detail. You can't buy that kind of attitude. I said, "We start in five days."

Outside the bank, Sam Winston flagged me down and asked if I still needed painters. Sam had moved to Clayoquot by mistake. A few summers earlier he had been living on the docks down in Trinidad when a huge black boat dropped anchor in the bay. It was Paul Watson's *Sea Shepherd*. They lured Sam aboard with tales of eco-piracy. Sail the seas. Save the world. Screw the Man.

It sounded good. He got his gear and found a bunk. Fifty miles out he realized the *Shepherd* was not a ship but a floating hundred-ton head game. It wasn't just Watson — everyone was at it, right down to the kitchen help, and they frittered so much energy on mental hockey that there was nothing left over to save the planet with.

The boat was an old Scottish freighter that was falling apart faster than the Soviet Union. Two hundred miles out they dropped anchor by mistake. The winch seized with the giant anchor suspended a hundred feet below the hull. They couldn't get to a harbour to fix it because the boat was now self-anchoring. No one knew what to do. They argued for hours. Days. Finally Sam took an acetylene torch and cut the chain, and the anchor plummeted to the ocean floor.

A month later they arrived in Tough City at the height of the Clayoquot blockades. It was a calm summer evening when that hulking black monster chugged into the channel. River and I climbed the hill behind the tennis courts to see what it was and watched George August paddle his canoe around the thing. Suddenly there was a deafening retort. Watson had fired his cannon to give the locals a heads-up. Hippies, rednecks and redskins were equally offended. It brought to mind the shelling of Opitsaht by the Yankee gunboat *Endeavor* back in 1867.

At the blockades Sam met a girl called Miriam, who had come to save the rainforest. He jumped ship and got work as a carpenter. Now he wanted to help paint the Floatel. I figured if he could handle life on the *Sea Shepherd,* he could survive a month up at Quait Bay.

The first trip up to Quait was the hardest. I was fine around the harbour buoys and along the shore in front of Opitsaht, but I got nervous as I approached the light in Maurus Channel because I wasn't sure what it meant. Around the light, water shoaled over flat rocks. The whole area made me tense. I had taken boats this far a hundred times, but this time, instead of heading across the channel at Robert Point towards Hippie Beach, I veered starboard. Soon I was farther into Bedwell Sound than I'd ever voyaged before. My mouth dried like a sand dollar. It seemed that at any moment I might feel the crunch of keel on rock, and all my hard work would be lost.

But I followed the charts, and an hour later I passed the scallop farm at the end of Cypress Bay. Up ahead the cliffs parted and I motored through a narrow channel into Quait. Beyond the cliffs the water was so calm that high tide had cut a razor line into the overhanging trees around the bay. I tied up at the dock and met with Erin and Gord, who managed the Floatel.

Those two were a typical Clayoquot couple. Gord was born in England among the pale and spotty, then emigrated to Australia and spent his boyhood running naked through the bush, killing birds with a catapult made from the fork of a branch and a scrap of tire rubber. After college he joined the UN and trained as a paratrooper, pulling fifty-man night jumps over the desert with a hundred pounds of gear. His first tour of duty was in Hong Kong, where Erin was dancing with a white tiger in the circus. When they got married they couldn't afford a house, so they bought a yacht instead, and it was moored to the Floatel dock.

That night I ate supper in the kitchen canyon. When I came down the ramp, Gord was sitting on the dock. "Listen."

The bay was alive with splashing. As my eyes adapted to the dark I saw thousands of salmon leaping from the water. So many were in the air at any given moment that they seemed frozen in mid-arc. The constant splashing sent a breeze across the dock that was so full of life I could taste it.

Next day I ran back to town to pick up the crew. I gradually got over my fear of finding an uncharted rock. The engine ran like a top. At the dock Art said, "I think that water in the crankcase was just rain that got blown down the stack. She's a good old boat."

On the return leg I chugged triumphantly past Hippie Beach. My naked pals waved at me. The knew me by my boat. I had become the skipper of the *Loch Ryan*.

My painting strategy was simple: we would start at one corner and keep going till we reached the end of the Floatel. It took five weeks and went off without a hitch, until the last week, when Gord climbed onto the roof to patch a hole. The ladder slipped out from under him and shot over the side, fell three storeys, bounced off the *Loch Ryan*'s roof, and disappeared into the water. That was Ralph's ladder. I had to get it back.

Gord had split his knee in the fall. That night we sat on his yacht and I watched him stitch his flesh back together with tools from his UN field kit. He said he had diving gear, but he couldn't go under with his knee cut up. "But you know how to dive, right, Andrew?"

It was true that I had chatted knowledgeably about diving with Gord a few days earlier, but in fact I had only been diving twice, and the first time didn't count. I got picked up hitchhiking near Nanoose, and the driver asked if I wanted to go "rock diving". I said, "What's that?" and he pulled over at the river canyon south of Nanaimo where the bungee jumpers plunge. He tossed me a mask and told me to grab a big rock from the riverbank. "Just let it pull you down," he said. I didn't know this guy from Adam, but I wasn't going to back out now. I took a deep breath and let the rock pull me into the depths until the glass in my mask creaked. The riverbed was flat, and there was a wrecked car sticking up out of the sand. I grabbed a root beer can to prove I'd reached bottom and swam back up towards the light. Later, at my sister's house in Victoria, I fell into a profound slumber that lasted fourteen hours. When I told my diver friend Jean Marc what I'd done, he said I was nuts. At any moment I might have blacked out from a burst eardrum and I'd still be down there. He took me out to the south tip of Vargas Island and showed me how to dive in a more professional manner.

We suited up on the deck of his yacht and toppled backward off the transom. Jean Marc waved his respirator. "When you want air, suck on this," he said. Then he put it in his mouth and motioned for me to follow. That's schooling, Clayoquot style.

We drifted down into a kelp forest. Wearing a weight belt underwater smacked of organized crime, and at first I was so nervous that my breathing came in huge gulps. But the kelp forest was peaceful, and the dappled light mesmerized me. After five minutes I forgot my fear and began to watch the creatures all around.

Unlike the tropics, which are a colourful undersea desert, the waters of Clayoquot Sound are full of life. The rocks were covered with purple urchins and orange starfish. Ghost shrimp like tiny glass lobsters drifted between fronds of kelp. A sea cucumber squirted past. I thought, Those things are weird. God must have been drunk when he made them. Fifteen minutes later I was stuffing urchins full of roe into a mesh sack when Jean Marc grabbed my flipper. He checked my air gauge and his eyes went round behind his mask. He made rapid chopping motions at his neck. My initial panic had caused me to breath so fast that I was already out of air. I made it to the surface just as the tank ran dry.

That had been the extent of my undersea education, but I told Gord, "No problem", got the gear on and toppled backwards off the gunnel of the *Loch Ryan,* trailing a rope. The bottom of the bay was a grim place. Gray mud undulated away into the gloom. I tied the rope to the ladder and yanked it, and the ladder picked itself up like a dead puppet and danced towards the light. The bay floor was nothing like the kelp forest off Vargas. The only place that was teeming with life was the underside of the *Loch Ryan.* I was mortified to see that her hull was a jungle of eelgrass and mussels. Moored next to her, Gord and Erin's hull was smooth as a baby's bottom. I had my next task cut out for me.

Three days before we finished, Jada-Lee began to miss Tom, so I went to town and got him. After work we soaked in the outdoor hot tub, then Tom and I jumped off the rail into the chuck. I asked Erin if we could jump off the second-floor deck. She nodded. "Just be careful you don't give yourself a chain wedgie on the anchor cables." Next we clambered onto the railing above the second-floor deck and leaped. Finally we climbed to the very top deck of the Floatel, and we were standing naked on the rail, psyching ourselves up for the terrible plunge, when Randy came round the point with a boatload of millionaire investors.

He was horrified. He barely noticed that we were all naked. He just kept staring at what was left of his Floatel — miles and miles of buckets and drop sheets and exposed electrical wiring. I told him it always looked darkest before the dawn. Two days later we had the place done up like a photo spread from *Architectural Digest.* Randy was overjoyed.

At sunset he met me down on Whitey's dock and cut me a cheque with enough zeros to pay off the crew and cover my chandlery tab. It was hard to believe that a month earlier the *Loch Ryan* wasn't even running.

I walked up the hill towards the bar. I was so distracted by all the zeros on my cheque that I rammed my head into the barricade, which had been lowered for the night. The blow almost knocked me out cold. I sat on a retaining wall and shook the bells from my skull. I felt dazed, but proud. I had managed to keep track of the Floatel's ten thousand parts without losing sight of the big picture. But Main Street looked all wrong. At first I thought I had been disoriented by that blow to the head. Then after a while I realized what it was. The old library was gone. While I was up at Quait Bay it had been torn down and turned into a parking lot.

FOUR

"IT'S GETTING IN SOMEWHERE," SAID LANCE AS
we watched the bilge pump come on again and spit a stream
of baccy juice out the side of the boat. I planned to find out
where when I put the *Loch Ryan* on the grid to careen the
hull, which is what they call it when you scrape away the carpets of mussels, barnacles, seaweed and tube worms that
flourish below the waterline.

The grid was a row of beefy wooden beams that lay
alongside the dock below Art's shed. Putting a boat on the
grid is pretty straightforward. At high tide you moor the
boat over the beams and wait until the water recedes. If
you've positioned the boat just right, she ends up balanced
on her keel. If you've positioned her wrong, she falls on her
side with a deafening crash and ends her days as matchwood. Fortunately, I had a rough idea of how it was done
because I had twice helped Crabber Dave put his boat, the
Scimitar, on the grid.

Crabber Dave was an Island boy. He grew up in Victoria,
a doctor's son, but he didn't think much of school. His two
loves were fishing and hockey. He was a Junior A hopeful,
NUMBER NINETEEN, with the big leagues snapping at his
skates. One night in Duncan he high-sticked the other
team's centre. After the play he skated over to apologize.

"I'm gonna cut out your eyes," said the centre. First chance he got he threw off his gloves and took Dave into the boards. The game ended in a rink-wide brawl, and Dave's team was trotted back to their bus through a gauntlet of cops, with the home crowd chanting, "KILL NINE-TEEN! KILL NINETEEN!"

After that he returned to his first love, fishing. He came to Clayoquot and got a job crabbing with Barry Grumbach. Something about it clicked. One afternoon he picked me up at Barry's house and we drove over to Gary Kolmus's, where a hundred crab traps were piled on the driveway.

"I bought the *Scimitar*," he said as we loaded the traps onto his truck. The *Scimitar* was a tight little double-ender, ideal for crabbing. First thing Dave did was put her on the grid. After we had her in position we sat on the dock and watched the stars, smoking cigarettes beside the big clam scale and listening to a guy who was loading a tote of live cod onto his truck: "I take them down the Island Highway and sell them to anyone I meet and if restaurants won't buy them hell I know I can always sell them to car dealers those guys are a sure sell they can't resist a deal it's like a disease can I bum one of those God it's a beautiful night . . ."

Once the water had drained away we scraped off all the vegetation, washed the hull and dried it with a tiger torch, which is basically a flame gun made from a propane tank and a length of rubber hose. Finally we wire-brushed the keel-cooler and painted everything with copper paint. At dawn, Dave's girlfriend showed up with sandwiches and beer. Dave drank his beer, cut the end off the can and slipped it over the big nut that held the *Scimitar*'s propellor in place. He melted a zinc bar with the tiger torch and poured it through a hole in the side of the can. When the zinc cooled it formed a sheath around the propellor nut that would keep electrolysis from eating away the metal.

Later we went crabbing up the inlet. It was a beautiful day, so after work we bought a flat of beer and Dave rounded up the Bottomfeeders, which was the band he played in. He ran the *Scimitar* up to God's Pocket and dropped anchor. Dave is a big guy with hands like hanks of sausage, but when he plays the mandolin he has the fingers of a doctor. John Armstrong, who is the actual doctor, played guitar. So did I. Pete Moffat played his fiddle, and Mike Thatcher thrummed away on his washtub base, which doubled as a giant ashtray for the whole band. The *Scimitar* drifted in lazy eights. Meares Island swung past, then Opitsaht, then Stone Island, then Meares again. Going round in circles never felt so good. I could see why Dave loved crabbing. So when Dick on the *Dark Star* asked around for a deckhand, I didn't hesitate.

On the first morning we headed south to Long Beach, where Dick had almost collided with a huge cement float the day before. He wanted to tow it home as salvage, but when we got to Comber's Beach we saw that it had been driven high onto the sand. Next we checked the traps in Florencia Bay. There was an octopus in one. Dick gutted and skinned it and put it in the bailing bucket. We drank coffee in the wheelhouse and talked about the cement float. It would be worth thousands if we could get it off the beach.

Back on deck we discovered the octopus had slithered out of the bucket and tried to escape through one of the scupper holes. I felt terrible. They say those things are as intelligent as cats. That night I took one of its tentacles over to Crabber Dave's house. He froze it, ran it through a meat grinder and made octopus burgers. They were delicious. Octopus seems an unlikely candidate for a redneck delicacy, but every old-timer had a secret recipe for eight-footed lasagna.

Next day Dick and I headed up to Hesquiat before dawn. It was so cold that the surface of Shelter Inlet was skimmed over with ice that shattered up around the prow as we ran. The rising sun made rainbows through it. He told me we were starting early so he could get "the jump" on someone who had been picking his traps.

Trap picking is the bane of crab fishermen. It drives them mad. They have to leave their line of traps for days at a time, and only the honesty of the group as a whole keeps them all above water. Dick said he'd come round Boulder Point a week earlier and there was a line of this other guy's traps right alongside his. "I seen him in the pub. I said, 'Ya fuckin' corked me!'"

Corking is where you lay a string of crab traps right alongside another crabber's. It's rude but not illegal. The problem is, when the lines are that close together it's hard to tell from afar which traps a crabber is pulling. Paranoia sets in, and next thing you know you've got a crab war on your hands.

The sky was clear and cold. There was no wind. Dick said, "I'm not afraid of him. I been in jail. I popped a wheelie right in front of the cops just to piss them off. Three hundred yards on one wheel. The judge said, 'That was a hell of a stunt, you should join some kind of circus.' I guess he meant stunt driving. But I never got the opportunity."

As we neared Hesquiat he came up with a plan. "I'll pull a couple of his traps, just to see how he's doing. If he's got nothing, then no biggie. But if he's got ten crabs a trap and I got squat, then I'll know for sure he's picking my traps, that son-of-a . . ."

The more he pictured the crime, the madder he got. He told me to take the wheel, went outside and kicked the bailing bucket around the deck. "An' while I got his traps on board, might as well take a couple of his crabs. Why not?

He's been taking mine!"

I could see how these crab wars got started. When we came around the point into Hesquiat there was a boat right beside a string of our floats. Dick thundered up alongside. It was Jamie Sloman, the most honest guy in town. He looked bewildered. Dick leaped up on the gunnel and motioned for me to back him up. I just waved, Jamie waved back, and that was the last time I went crabbing for Dick. It seemed the whole fishery was set up to induce paranoia and distrust of your fellow man. Crabber Dave agreed. He told me they had video cameras on the traps up at Hecate Strait now.

When I told him I was putting the *Loch Ryan* on the grid, he gave me his tiger torch and a long-handled tool for scraping the barnacles off the bottom. I motored round to the grid, tied up to some pilings and waited for the tide to drop. Low tide was at six in the morning. I fell asleep in the fo'c's'le listening to the weather radio. At dawn Art Clarke came stomping down the dock and hollered, "Where is he? That boat's gonna go over!"

I scrabbled on deck, blinking like a mole-rat. The boat had settled on a slight tilt away from the pilings. Only the ropes I had tied to the dock held her upright. "Hurry!" yelled Art. "Jesus! She's good as matchwood! I might as well call the backhoe!"

"What do I do?"

"Tie that rope from the mast over to the pilings!"

My heart tried to beat its way out of my chest as I worked. My shirt where it touched the hollow of my throat was cold with sweat. "What next?"

"Oh, she'll be fine now." He went inside to brew the coffee for the Fishermen's Club.

Putting a boat on the grid is like therapy. It costs a fortune, takes forever, and you find all sorts of stuff below the surface that you just don't want to deal with. There was a three-inch carpet of mussels on the hull. They came off in hoary swathes, and by noon the tide was back in and I was black as a licorice twist. On the next tide I had her balanced better, tilted slightly towards the pilings. I dried the wood with the tiger torch, rolled on two coats of paint, and replaced the zincs, which had crumbled to gray sludge. I tapped a waxy hempen material called oakum between the keel and the larboard plank, where it looked like water might be getting in. But when the tide rose, the bilge pump came on and stayed on. Where was the water coming from?

Art said there was no hole in the hull. "Never has been. That's a good old boat." He pointed out an assemblage of giant nuts where the engine shaft went through the hull. It was called the stuffing box. The nuts had to be slightly loose so that the shaft could turn freely, so it always leaked a little. But it shouldn't be leaking this much. There was a hemp washer between the nuts that might need changing.

I went to Whitey's and bought a giant red pipe wrench that looked like a cartoon murder weapon, waited for the tide to drop again, backed off the two fist-sized nuts around the shaft, changed the hemp washer and snugged them back up. When the tide rose, the bilge pump kept quiet. Another moment of victory. I sat on the gunnel, spent, watching the waves lap around the freshly painted hull. Now that I could see her lines I realized they were elegant. An old shipwright from Oregon gave me the thumbs-up from the dock.

"She's a beaut. Couldn't build a hull like that today for a hundred grand."

"Oh yes," said Art, leaning over the rail. "That's Sam Eadie's boat. Old Sammy loved his boat. It was like his pet."

He told me Sam Eadie had owned the boat before Derek Arnet. Sammy was a five-foot Norseman who came to Clayoquot back in the fifties to escape from his wife, a big woman who never stopped talking. Sammy craved solitude and silence. For ten years he fished alone on a double-ender called the *Daisy*.

Early one morning in 1966 he was tied up beside Len Clay in Nuchatlitz Harbour. Both planned to run down the coast that day. They had coffee together, then Len took his boat out through the channel, and when he put on his glasses to check the chart he couldn't see a thing. He had grabbed Sammy's glasses by mistake. Meanwhile, Sammy was five miles out to sea. Just before dawn he noticed *Daisy* was helming funny. When he looked back he couldn't see anything. When he finally opened the door to get a better look the sea flooded over the sill into the wheelhouse. Freshwater had wicked along the horn beam in *Daisy*'s timbered stern to the rudder stem, which was made from two-inch pipe. It had rusted through and snapped, leaving a hole the size of a dollar coin in the horn beam, through which the sea now poured.

Sammy brought her round to port and ran for shore. Water gushed over the bulkhead and swirled up the side of the engine. Four miles out he knew he wasn't going to make it. He had no dinghy and no life jacket. He couldn't even swim.

With water foaming up his shins he lashed a couple of empty fuel cans together and grabbed a shear pig, which is a float that shears a trolling line away from the back of a salmon boat. They're called shear pigs because they were once made from the inflated hide of a pig, although Sammy had replaced his with Styrofoam. Moments later the boat sucked down right beneath his feet. What a terrible way to start the day. One minute he was drinking coffee, the next he was bobbing like a squeeze toy as the sun rose over a lonely sea, and nothing for miles except shearwaters and albatross wheeling above the flotsam of his life.

That water was cold. Sammy knew he didn't have long to live. Just when he thought things couldn't get any worse, a flock of seagulls settled around his head and he realized they probably wouldn't wait till he was dead before they started pecking. Another boat running down the coast saw the gulls congregating. The skipper paid it no heed, but his wife was aboard, and she kept at him till he deviated from his course just to get some peace. When they fished Sammy onto the deck he had been in the water for half an hour. He had come to Clayoquot to escape his wife's nagging, and now nagging had saved his life. All he had left were his clothes and Len Clay's glasses. He started from scratch, bought the *Loch Ryan* a year later and fished her until he was seventy, trolling for salmon with his lines rigged to wooden poles that had cowbells hung on them. When a salmon tugged on a line, the bells would ring. He could tell from the tone of the bell how big the fish was.

One morning he set his gear and charted a course down the coast to Long Beach. It was chilly, so he cranked the diesel stove, made some coffee and dozed off in the warm wheelhouse. When he woke up the bells were ringing like it was Easter Sunday. He thought he'd hit Fish Vegas until he looked out the window and saw he was a hundred yards from shore, in water ten feet deep. The bells were ringing because his gear was trundling along the bottom. He took it as a sign that it was time to retire and sold the *Loch Ryan* to Derek Arnet.

I was happy that I owned such a tasty chunk of Tough City history. And the old girl had life in her yet. The hull was clean and the tanks were full, and I was ready to explore the Sound. I decided not to worry about the monthly payments in the offing. I would just relax and enjoy the summer with my amazing boat.

First place on my hit list was Hippie Beach, a string of sandy bays that stretched beneath the old copper mine on Catface Mountain. My friend Cal Kalkan had built a cabin on one of them. Cal was born in a remote Turkish village. He got his first toothache at ten, and they sent him to the horse doctor. He watched sun glint off the giant metal pliers as the old man reached into his mouth and yanked the tooth out painlessly. Amazing — except it was the wrong tooth. The old man tried again, and the rotten tooth broke into pieces. Cal was furious. He figured he was cut out for finer things than sharing his dentist with a horse. He wanted to be an artist. He joined the Turkish navy, hoping to apprentice as a draughtsman, but they made him a torpedo mechanic and trained him as an electrician. They also thrashed him regularly, so first chance he got he fled to Canada, where he had two daughters, paid the bills by working as an electrician in Tough City, and dreamed of a time when he would spend his days drawing and painting. When his daughters were grown he got Joe Martin to fell a couple of big hemlocks out on Hippie Beach, and the following summer I helped him Alaska-mill them into lumber. Now the lumber was a cabin with stained glass windows and half-finished canvases everywhere.

I didn't have a runabout yet, so I dropped anchor in the bay and swam ashore. When I reached Cal's cabin there was a regular hootenanny happening. Frank Harper, editor of the local paper, had dropped by for tea. Cal had laid some books of Renaissance paintings on the bed, and Godfrey Stephens was chainsawing into a big block of cedar from Cal's woodshed.

Godfrey grew up in what is now Goldstream Park, just

outside of Victoria, back when there were no rules of any kind. I have a photograph of him at age twelve, with a dozen guns laid out on his bed. In the fifties he moved to San Francisco to hang out with the beatniks. One night they all went to a Matisse show at the art gallery. When he saw the famous nudes he wasn't impressed. "I can do better tits than that," he told his pals. He was right. He had an uncanny gift when it came to lines. Soon he was able to travel around the world, trading art for food and shelter. Princess Anne got one of his carvings, the king of Nepal got one of his paintings, and every time he sold a piece of art he put the money into a new boat.

For Godfrey, the most important part of building a boat was putting in a porthole below the waterline. Then he would get his latest girlfriend to dive under the boat and swim around like a mermaid while he rattled off sketches of her impossibly lithe and lovely form. While Cal and I argued about the meaning of art, Godfrey took a hook knife and sliced at the cedar block until the head of a woman emerged. By suppertime he was cutting the fine details of her features. By bedtime he was sanding out the knife marks. We lay on our backs and talked, looking up at the light cast across the ceiling. Even the curving patches of shadow above us seemed to conceal the limbs of mermaids.

Next morning Cal made oatmeal for breakfast, and Godfrey gobbled his standing up so he could keep rubbing oil into his sculpture. Cal took me out to the *Loch Ryan* in his canoe. I ran her back to town, slept for an hour, then went for lunch at the Alleyway Cafe. Godfrey's bust was sitting on the picnic table outside. "I sold it!" he cried when he saw me. "Five grand!" He tied a bandana on his head, rolled a cigarette and began quoting Coleridge.

Hippie Beach had worked out so well that I decided to

try for Hot Springs Cove, a few miles farther up the coast. My friend Steve asked if he and his girlfriend Cynthia could come along. Steve baked the bread at the Common Loafer and Cynthia worked at the fish plant. They had hooked up the summer before when I took them both skydiving. Now they were going to have a baby, for which I felt vaguely responsible. How could something like that happen twice?

We ran up Millar Channel past Ahousaht, the largest Native village in Clayoquot. In 1864 the crew of the trading schooner *Kingfisher* were killed in a sortie with the Ahousaht chief Cap-chah. British Rear Admiral Denman sailed up Matilda Inlet in a gunboat and demanded the Ahousahts surrender their chief. The Ahousahts said that Denman should come and take him.

The limeys shelled villages and burned canoes while Cap-chah led the resistance clad in a blue Navy jacket taken from an officer on the *Kingfisher.* For days they played hide-and-seek along the shore, then Denman left for Victoria, promising he'd be back in a month with more guns. But for reasons unknown he never returned. Cap-chah's star rose as the great chief who kicked King George's ass, and the memory of that early victory lingers. Ahousaht still feels like a place that has never surrendered.

Beyond the village we chugged through Sulphur Passage to Shelter Inlet, then past the mouth of Sydney Inlet to Baseball Bay. We called it that because years earlier fishermen discovered they could pick up radio signals from America when they anchored there. They would tie up in rafts on summer evenings and listen to ball games coming through the ether from San Francisco. In the forest above the bay was a wooden palisade, all that remained of the ancient Nu-chah-nulth capital of Opnit. Around the point from the ruins, a hot spring flowed over a rock ledge and down through a crevice into the waves. My plan was to run around Sharp Point, tie up at the government dock in Hot Springs Cove and spend the night soaking in the springs.

The sea was calm until we reached the outside swell, and then waves the size of haystacks began to hit the boat from all directions. Food flew from galley shelves. Books hit the stove. It wasn't pretty. But Steve and Cynthia trusted me completely. They sat on the roof of the wheelhouse and whooped as I struggled to keep us afloat. The *May Queen,* a big old cod boat, ran alongside us with the tattered black flags of her traps flapping in the wind. When we got to Sharp Point the *May Queen* ran out to open water. She was going around the can buoy. I wanted to stick close to her in case I got into trouble, but that can buoy was halfway to Japan, and I was already terrified. The waves out there were smashing together in terrific explosions of foam and spray. I decided to round the point the way I always had on smaller boats — snugged up against the rocks.

The next wave picked up the *Loch Ryan* and tossed her sideways into a trough so deep I couldn't see the shore. I heard Steve and Cynthia holler with glee from the roof. Little did they know I was locked in a life-or-death arm-wrestle with the ship's wheel. I could hear the chain gear slipping, *chunk! chunk! chunk!* as we slid into another trough. We dropped down and down, so close to the rocks that I could make out individual strands of kelp, with white water running down between them in rivulets. I thought it was the end of me. I gunned the engine, but the prop seemed to come right out of the water. Then I felt the boat being lifted up, and we surfed down the face of the next wave into the mouth of Hot Springs Cove.

The wind died to nothing and the water flattened out. It was hard to believe that this was the same day. No wonder we called the place Refuge Cove, until the Feds stepped in and reminded everyone that Refuge Cove was a place on the West Redonda Island in the Inside Passage. Art Clarke's dad, Ivan, certainly found Hot Springs to be a refuge when he waited out a storm there with forty other boats back in 1938. The outside waters were sheer madness, but the cove was like a lake. A packer loaded with groceries made it round Sharp Point and sold everything aboard in minutes. Ivan was impressed. He returned a year later and built the Hot Springs General Store with lumber salvaged from an old copper mine up Stewardson Inlet.

I tied up at the dock and watched the *May Queen* struggle through the chop. When she tied up behind me the deckhand said, "You got balls of steel. Weren't you worried about the rock pile?"

"Nah," I said. Then I went inside and checked the chart. I had overlooked a star at the mouth of the cove. I had slid blindly between the point and a submerged rock. I asked the deckhand if that was why the can buoy lay so far out. He nodded, and I made a mental note to ask such questions ahead of time in the future.

When I first began visiting the hot springs there was never anyone around. Wearing a bathing suit seemed wrong, like a bear on a bicycle. Then the Feds built changing rooms at the top of the slope. Next time I visited the springs they were packed, and I hadn't even brought a suit. I slipped into the water hoping no one would notice. A skinny guy wearing jeans and smoking a filter tip scowled at my lack of propriety. Then he tossed his filter into the water, and it was my turn to scowl. At least I carried out everything I brought in. The incident had sullied the innocence of the place, but now with the *Loch Ryan* I could stay overnight. At dusk, when we wandered up the boardwalk to the springs, they were deserted, as they had been in the old days.

We rolled some rocks together to make a pool and lay there while the tide came in. After a few hours my face was frozen while my back boiled like soup bones. I felt utterly relaxed. But I couldn't shake the image of coming down hard on that rock pile. The terrifying shatter of limbs and boards, the sizzle of hot engine parts on the face of the deep — and then nothing. Vanished without a trace. On the upside, I knew the *Loch Ryan* could handle anything.

Back in town I decided a boat this good should look the part, which she didn't. There were six coats of lumpy paint on the trim. I bought a grinder at the Co-op and chewed my way down to the original wood through coats of brown, blue, white and bright orange. Underneath that scabrous sheath was beautiful teak, gumwood and brass. I dismantled the drop windows and rebuilt them. I polished the brass and painted the hull. By the time I was done, so was summer, and the *Loch Ryan* was a babe. I couldn't believe it. How did I end up with a boat like this? Every joint, every board was perfectly made.

I asked Art who built her. He didn't know. All he remembered was that she had been a double-ender until Sam Eadie had her stretched at Wingen's shipyard. I had never heard of a shipyard in town, but Art said to go look under Whitey's dock. When I leaned over the rail I saw what appeared to be train tracks running into the waves below, like the tail end of the National Dream. It was the old marine track, where shipwrights once pulled boats out of the sea to work on them. Those rusted rails were all that remained of T. H. Wingen and Son, once the third-largest shipyard on Vancouver Island.

Tom Wingen came through the Graveyard in 1903 and found work at Mosquito Cove on the north shore of Meares

Island. Today Meares is an icon of untouched nature, but in Tom's day there was a sawmill at Mosquito that employed forty men. They logged the land between Meares and Kennedy Lake, chartered a freighter and sent a million board feet of shingles round the tip of South America to buyers in New York. The ship arrived on the East River just as the economy collapsed, and the mill shut down.

Suddenly unemployed, Tom built his own mill and blacksmith's shop at Indian River, salvaging the timber and steel he needed from wrecks he found on Long Beach. For power he built a dam and a water wheel. He sold the lumber he milled to the men of Opitsaht, who used it to build their houses. In 1920 he built the first modern boat in Clayoquot Sound, the *Tofino*. He cut the wood at his mill, made the fittings in his blacksmith's shop, and used wooden runners to get her in and out of the water.

When Hillmar, son of Tom, reached school age, the family moved down the inlet to where Tofino stands today. At that time it was wilderness. Most of town still lay across the water on Stubbs Island. Tom and Hillmar built three vessels, the *Ave Maria,* the *Charlene* and the *Kumtuks*. In 1929 Hillmar opened T. H. Wingen's Machine Shop. Over the next decade he set up a blacksmith shop for his dad and added a mill and a boat house.

This was back when the only source of supplies from the outside world was the *Princess Maquinna*. If the Wingens needed something fast, they had to make it themselves, so out of necessity they built their boats from whatever was at hand.

For the hulls they used red cedar, *Thuja plicata,* which was unknown in Norway, and is not really cedar — it got its name because it smells like the cedars of Lebanon, a wood so costly in the Old World that it was used only to line chests. But in the New World the Wingens were surrounded by the stuff, and it made excellent boats so long as it was cut properly. In winter they went into the forest and carved deep grooves all the way round the trunks of the trees they wanted. In spring the sap couldn't rise, so the wood became rot-resistant. They cut the logs into cants at the new mill and left them to dry in the shed for a year.

Cedar made good planking, but it was not strong enough to make keels. For that they needed fir. The Clayoquot is so temperate that fir rarely grows at sea level. They had to salvage trees that came down from the mountains above Kennedy Lake in winter landslides.

For ribs they tried western yew. Hillmar's first experiment, a tugboat called the *Qiuodgar*, had solid yew ribs, but the first time the shipwrights tried to replace a plank they couldn't get the nails back out. Next he tried laminate ribs made from thin strips of yellow cedar and yew, which held and released nails well and were so elastic that you could bounce a boat off the rocks like a tennis ball.

By now the Wingens were pouring their own bearings and rebuilding engines from the block up — pistons, heads, rods — right out of raw metal. Just before the War, Hillmar built a two-stroke gas engine from scratch. He turned the crankshaft on a lathe, but it never really worked, so he gave it up. They continued to build gurdies, fittings and machine parts until the sixties, when Bob, son of Hillmar, invented the stabilizer, a weighted fin that hangs on a pole from a vessel's sides and makes BC fish boats look like giant mosquitoes on the water.

Bob was a genius. By the age of six he was exploring the Sound in his own runabout. When he turned thirteen, Hillmar gave him a fish boat he'd just finished and told him to take her round to Vancouver. Bob was barely tall enough to see over the wheel. He took a chart, a compass and a round sight glass for navigation. He set his course on the chart, laid the sight glass along it and rolled it over to the compass to get his bearing. He ran the boat down through the Graveyard and into the Port of Vancouver without a hitch.

When he got home, Hillmar gave him a second boat to take round and told him to be careful because War had broken out in Europe. Bob didn't know where Europe was, but he knew it was a lot farther than Vancouver, so he didn't worry. He reached Juan de Fuca Strait in the dead of night. Suddenly the wheelhouse was flooded with unearthly light. It was an American coastguard cutter, trolling for Japanese two years before Pearl Harbor.

"Where's the skipper?"

"I'm the skipper."

"Where's the real skipper?"

They refused to believe a boy of thirteen had taken a boat through the Graveyard. They grilled him for an hour before they let him go. When he made Victoria, the Canadian Navy boarded him and ran him through the same ordeal.

But on the whole the War was good to the Wingens. While the big shipyards in Vancouver and Victoria were tied up with the war effort, the Wingens couldn't keep up with the work they got building and rebuilding the fishing fleet. At the peak there were forty-five men working in the shipyard. They built twenty-six new boats and rebuilt dozens more. They had one man just tapping oakum, that oily material made from hemp soaked in paraffin that I'd used to caulk the seams in the *Loch Ryan*'s hull. There was a finish carpenter building cabinets for the wheelhouses, and half a dozen machinists working on the engines and running gear.

Wingen boats were famous up and down the coast because each was unique. At night a fisherman would come in to Hillmar's study, and they would drink coffee and talk about hulls for hours. Hillmar would get some three-quarter-inch slats and nail them together, then whittle away until he got the shape of the hull just the way the fisherman wanted. Then he pulled the slats apart, laid them on paper and traced them to get the lines. Next, Bob would loft the hull, laying out a full-size copy of the plan on the boat house floor so he could rig up the skeleton: keelson, forefoot, bow board, stringers, ribs, planking. There were six shipwrights, all Norsemen, and four of them were Bob's uncles. They couldn't read or write, but they could lay down a board and cut the end to shape with a broadaxe, and it would fit into the forefoot like a hand in a glove.

After the War the work dropped off, so they took contracts building and rebuilding seiners. The largest vessel they built was a sixty-five–foot seiner for Hildegards in Ucluelet. They had a new head shipwright, Doug Busswood, who had been stationed at the airport during the War and stayed to build boats, and could swing a sledgehammer against a boat nail in a continuous circle, roundhouse — *ching! ching! ching!* like he was playing a big one-note piano.

When Whitey Bernard arrived in 1961 the machine shop looked like a living museum of west coast nautical know-how. The boilers were salvaged from shipwrecks. The tools were powered by belts that raced between the rafters overhead. When Whitey wanted to run the planer or the drill he had to engage the belt above it. The whole shop got turned on in the morning and ran till the whistle blew at five.

By this time half of town was wired to Wingen's. On Friday nights Bob would put an extra gallon in the generator, and the houselights stayed on until 10:30. If they were having a good time, Doug would go down the hill and add a second gallon, which kept them going past midnight. Inside the door he kept a barrel of yew wood blocks pickling in brine. When a fisherman wanted a new stern bearing, Whitey would machine one out of yew. A metal bearing cost fifty bucks and made a hum that scared away the fish, but a yew wood bearing was free, and quiet to boot. The only drawback was an indelible purple dye that came out of the wood. Even this was put to use. When Doug hired a new man he'd send him to fish a block out of the barrel, and his arm would come out purple. It took weeks to wash off. He had to walk around town with a purple arm, and everyone knew he was the new man at Wingen's.

One summer the new man was Don McGinnis. He had been building houses in town and was keen to give boat building a try. He bust his butt for two weeks and was mortified to find he couldn't fasten more than three planks a day. On the last day Bob and Doug found him packing his things.

"Where are you going?"

"I'm quitting before I get fired."

They laughed and laughed. A plank a day is pretty good. Three planks is unheard of. They made him foreman. Don was skeptical, but Doug said it would work like hot damn. "I hate telling people what to do," he said, "and you don't."

The first boat Don worked on was the *Loch Ryan*. Sam Eadie wanted the stern stretched and flattened to make the cockpit roomier for trolling. He also had rolling chocks put on to make her more stable in a following sea. I asked Don where Sammy got the boat, but he didn't know. He had an inkling that she was once called by another name, but he couldn't remember what it was. Now I was hooked. I had pushed the history of the *Loch Ryan* back a generation, yet still the mystery deepened.

One night I dreamed I had the *Loch Ryan* in such good shape that I was able to trade her to Chris for the *Oldfield.*

Pasheabel's new cabin was the size of a school gym. But when I looked down through the hatch, water was pouring onto her bed. Below decks looked like a junkyard. I thought, Oh, why did I do this? Art Clarke stood at the top of the ramp, shaking his head. "Andrew, get her fixed up or get her out of here!" I ran down the ramp with a paintbrush. The *Oldfield* was now the size of the *Queen Elizabeth*. I didn't know where to start. The bilge pump came on and she rolled onto her side with a tremendous boom, then righted herself, and four great geysers of oily water fired out of giant portals along the hull, smashing the dock to smithereens.

When I awoke I still owned the *Loch Ryan*. I was so happy. I realized that I loved my boat. I wondered how many people had felt that way over the years. A boat as old as the *Loch Ryan* touches so many lives she becomes like a river system that connects whole landscapes. I wanted to track the river to its source. I had found the boat papers in the nook next to the engine manual, but they cast no light on her past. Builder: UNKNOWN. Port of origin: UNKNOWN. She was a mystery.

FIVE

"THIS IS THE LIFE!" SAID PASHEABEL. SHE WAS down in the fo'c's'le cabin, curled up on her bunk with her new puppy, Zeus, on her lap, buried under blankets and reading *The Lord of the Rings*.

Up in the wheelhouse I lay on my bunk with a book of my own. I had almost finished the complete works of Jung when he took a huge detour into seventeenth-century alchemy. His theory was that the alchemists, in their quest to turn lead into gold, had confused chemistry with metaphysics. The transformation was supposed to be a metaphor for enlightenment. I found his theory interesting, but it went on for hundreds of pages. Pretty soon it was like watching a super-intelligent dog chase its own tail until it fell on its side.

A lot of Jung's books had been edited by the American scholar Joseph Campbell, so I started reading his stuff. His central tenet was that God was a metaphor for something you could never pin down, and people got confused because they tried to render the divine into something concrete. It sounded a little abstract, but I found out Campbell had been the fastest runner in North America while he was in college. His theories were a marriage of brains and sweat. I figured I could trust him to keep it real.

As the red tail lights of summer faded I began to regret

my decision not to pay off the *Loch Ryan* with the booty from the Floatel gig. Late with September's moorage, I chugged over to the crab dock, where there was no electricity, so I figured it must be a lot cheaper than Fourth Street. It was certainly a lot quieter. One morning I washed dishes in the galley and stared at the gunmetal belly of cloud that stretched across the inlet to Meares Island. The oil stove was cranked and the wheelhouse felt cozy as the stub end of a nap. I had ordered all of Joseph Campbell's books from Linda, who was now ensconced in the new library building. They were lined up on the shelf above the ship's wheel. I wanted to curl up and read until spring, but unlike the last seven winters, the one ahead was mined with boat payments. I had to get a job.

Whenever I wanted work the first place I looked was Stubbs, an island that lay west of the harbour mouth in the middle of Father Charles Channel. Until World War II, half of Tofino was on Stubbs. At first I thought it strange that the settlers had built town straddling a body of water. That's because I was looking at it from the land. Tough City is like Bamfield — it only makes sense if you look at it from the water. Until 1959 there was no road here. Everything travelled by boat. So in the beginning, water was not a barrier. It was the connective tissue.

When the *mamaalthi* settlers arrived, the sand spit on Stubbs was dotted with stakes, upon which grinned the skulls of thirty Kuyuquot braves. They had been decapitated by the warrior chief Cal-Cum. They would spend the afterlife with their faces on their chests and descend to a longhouse under their village where they would live on charcoal and salmon.

Unfazed by all the skulls, a man named Pinney built a chandlery on the spit in 1854. He lit a huge driftwood beacon at the end, hoping to lure ships in from the outside channel, but not one bit. Ten years later, Freddy Thornberg came around Cape Hope on a schooner called the *Black Knight* and jumped ship in Victoria. The schooner took on a load of boat spars, sailed for Alaska and vanished without a trace. Thornberg bought Dawley's old chandlery and threw out all the rusted chain and anchors. He propped a shotgun under the counter and started trading with the Indians through a hole in a giant cedar slab. Soon the wood was shredded with buckshot from deals gone sour, but the clientele wouldn't kill Freddy because he was kin, having married a Nuu-chah-nulth woman named Lucy. They ran the place together for fifty years.

In 1872 he arranged for the braves of the nearby village of Kelsemaht to go seal hunting on a Danish schooner. They set out on rough January waves and vanished without a trace. Only two Kelsemaht men survived, because they had been ill when the schooner came through. They knew their women and children would starve that winter. It was the end of their nation. They smashed the big cedar slab at the trading post and prepared to kill Freddy. He talked them out of it by negotiating relief with the British government. Each Kelsemaht woman would receive a sack of flour, a pound of tea and a blanket on the first of every month. He thought they might trade these goods for fish and oil. But on the day the shipment arrived, people came from miles around and the women shared out everything they had, as was their wont. Next morning they showed up at Thornberg's trading hole looking for more.

Despite these woes, the trading post prospered. By the turn of the century there were buildings all along the waterfront and a big harbour lantern on a floating platform to warn ships away from the sand spit.

After the Great War the harbour light was tended by an English recluse named Frederick Tibbs. As a child he fell on a spindle that left a hole through the side of his face, and from this fairytale wound his shyness grew, until even Clayoquot wasn't far enough away from people.

Fred lived alone out on Dream Island in a hand-hewn wooden castle with a rose garden under the window. He wrote his niece in the Old Country that his dream was to transform a "wild, rugged patch of forest into a little bit of England." To this end he cut down all the trees on the island except for a hundred-foot spruce, which he limbed and topped with a scaffold. At dawn he would climb to the top and play reveille on a cornet. In July 1921 he blasted himself with some dynamite while trying to remove a rock from his island paradise. Already sick, he exhausted himself further fighting a fire that had engulfed the hotel on Stubbs. Next morning he rowed out to tend the harbour light. While he was pouring coal oil into the reservoir his boat slipped off the float and drifted away towards Opitsaht.

Fred was a strong swimmer, so he stripped down and swam after it. Before he got halfway, an Opitsaht man came by in a motor launch and took the boat in tow, unable to hear Fred shouting over the engine. Now he was alone in the middle of the channel. He swam towards Stubbs and made it to the big rock off the end of the spit, where he stood naked, flapping his arms, until three Native women digging clams on the beach sent a little boy for help. The town doctor hoofed along the spit, but by the time he arrived, Fred was dead on the sand. He had tried to reach shore and become tangled in the eelgrass.

Like those headless Kuyuquot warriors, Fred went down below the sand spit and continued his life's work underground. We know this because later the village gathered up its trusses and waded across the channel to the mainland, and the old townsite became a grassy meadow with flower beds and spreading broadleaf trees, the part of Clayoquot Sound that most resembles the little bit of England in Fred's dream.

In the twenties Bill White, still a lad, got work showing an American the best tide pools on the island's outer coast. The American collected specimens of marine life and sold them to biology departments in Stateside universities. His name was Ed Ricketts, and he shows up as Doc in Steinbeck's *Cannery Row*. Canneries had sprung up in every bay along the coast down to California. There were eleven in Clayoquot Sound alone, built for the pilchard, a kind of giant sardine. In 1931 they canned 160,000 tons of pilchard. Such fortunes waited to be made that one entrepreneur floated a whole cannery on a barge up to Sydney Inlet, along with thirty young women from Glasgow to work the line. That's why we call the end of Holmes Inlet Pretty Girl Cove.

The next year there was not a pilchard to be found. The fishery shut down, and Holmes Inlet became a place where fishermen could get blown ashore. When I heard about the Steinbeck connection I wondered if the denizens of Pretty Girl had inspired the hookers of Cannery Row, wherein a Californian cannery becomes a bordello after the sardine fishery collapses.

To this day no one knows where the pilchard went. Overfishing is the popular theory, but if that had been the case, surely one or two stragglers would have shown up in the following years. All we know for certain is that the pilchard is an odd fish. If you leave one in a bowl on the wood stove overnight, by morning there's just the tail and a pool of oil.

When the fishery collapsed there was so much pilchard oil in abandoned cannery tanks around Tofino that people added pigment to the stuff and used it to paint their houses. That must have smelled good. Joe Martin once gave me a can of oil from a drift whale that came ashore near Opit-saht. I oiled a fir beam at my pyramid as an experiment. It added a rich lustre to the wood and a foul stench to the air that grew stronger with each passing day. I used linseed oil on the rest of the beams, and it's a good thing too, because I could smell the stench from that single whale-oiled patch well into spring. I guess when we romanticize the past we forget how it must have reeked.

After the pilchard debacle, a Japanese fisherman named Kimoto built a house on Stubbs. He had been living with his family in an abandoned hotel on Stockham Island, but he hated it because every night the ghost of an old Indian woman would come upstairs and try to strangle him. Soon there was a whole Japanese village on Stubbs. Each family had its own boat. They were master fishermen, and they taught the white settlers how to troll for salmon. One night Kimoto got tangled in his anchor line and drowned. It seemed like a bad omen, and it was. When Canada went to war in 1942, all the Japanese trollers were seized, taken round to Steveston harbour, moored in a flotilla, and sold for as little as a dollar. At the library I found a picture of them all boomed together near New Westminster. Their hulls looked a lot like the *Loch Ryan*'s. Perhaps she was war spoils, and this was why no record of her existed before 1950.

After the War, Stubbs Island became a quiet place. In the sixties, Lana Gibson spent an afternoon playing near the abandoned village with a little Japanese girl. It turned out she was a ghost. Her mother had drowned her in the bay because she was ugly. Years later the woman had another daughter, a pretty girl. They were fishing in the bay one morning when a silver perch swam under the boat. "Lean over and look at the beautiful fish!" said the woman. "Okay," said the pretty girl, "but this time don't push me in."

The jail, hotel, post office and long wooden trestle with train tracks on top that curved along the waterfront slowly fell into ruin. By the time I arrived, most of the buildings were gone, except for the hotel, which stood at the edge of the water, a big square relic from settlers' days. One morning after a winter storm I looked across the freezing whitecaps from the Whiskey Dock and saw that the outbuilding of the hotel had collapsed during the night and was sloping drunkenly towards the water. For the next few months there was work on the island, tearing down the lodge and cleaning up the sand spit.

That same winter, down on Saltspring Island, a big guy called Chris had landed a plum job looking after a mansion. The place had its own beach and dock, and he loved it. One afternoon an American heiress landed in a float plane. She said her name was Susan Bloom, she had seen the mansion from the plane, she loved the look it and she was going to buy it. Chris phoned the owner in a panic. "Is it true?" The owner just laughed. "Never in a million years."

Two weeks later Chris carried Susan's bags up the dock. That summer they flew over Stubbs and Susan loved the look of it, too. She bought the whole island with the intent of turning it into a wilderness preserve, and left Chris to hire a crew and get the transformation underway. I was on that crew. We raised buildings, put in flower beds, and built boardwalks that led everywhere. It was good work and paid well. My hope was that there would be more work on Stubbs that winter, so I ran the *Loch Ryan* past Round Island and tied up at the dock. I found Chris putting bat guano on his winter potatoes. He said there was no work at all on the island, but did I want a homemade beer?

We wandered back to the dock and sat looking across the channel towards town. "What about over there?" he said. "They're building like madmen." It was true. From the dock we could see the pine ribcage of a new house rising from the trees near Harold Monk's place. I motored back to town and asked around at the Common Loafer. Laser Dave's brother Mike had just begun building his house out towards Grice Bay. The contractors were the Sadler brothers, Kenny and Harold, and Kenny's partner John Bradford. Together they helmed Tough City's Christian Right.

They say angels fly in circles because there's no left wing in heaven, but the Sadlers thought outside the box. They drove around with giant ALLIANCE stickers on their trucks, yet they practised a radical form of socialism where everyone shared like brothers. Right now they were madly building houses for each other in a muskeg flatland near Mackenzie Beach that some wag had dubbed Ned Flanders Fields. They hired me on the spot, with the proviso that I never cuss on the work site.

The Sadlers built every house from scratch — foundation, frame, siding, roof, floors, cabinets. They had each job figured out like a game. Kenny's favourite was laying the foundation. The whole house had to be square within a millionth of an inch, and then he was a happy man. My favourite was siding. Kenny cut the boards on a pull saw and tossed them up to the scaffold, where Harold and I caught them out of the air like baseballs.

Those boys were so ready to be swept up into the clouds that they scorned gravity. Their dad, Jim Sadler, was famous for his surfing exploits and infamous for running along underfoot and yanking the nails out of the scaffold supports while the crew was still dismantling the planks above. One time the whole shebang came down and Sadlers went flying left and right, Wallenda-style. Kenny broke his back, but Jim escaped injury by landing on another guy. The man suffered from a condition known as horseshoes. Elders in Victoria still talk about the time he slid off the roof of the church while standing on a sheet of plywood and surfed it down three storeys to the lawn. He even managed a bottom turn.

The Sadlers were unnerved by how well I knew the Bible. They were used to scientific arguments against creationism, not theological ones. They were outraged yet amused when I called the Bible "Windows 33 AD". Some afternoons Harold and I went at it so long that Kenny begged us to stop talking about God. "Guys! We have a house to build!"

But I was incorrigible. I loved talking about God. I was raised Christian, the grandson of a Protestant minister. As a kid I dreamt constantly about the Final Judgement. God looked like my grandad, and I would help him pitch souls into hell and pray he would go easy on me when he twigged that I was one of the damned. After all, we were family.

When we came to Canada, everything was different. My folks fell to feuding with their minister, who stole money from the collection plate and blamed my mum. After my dad got over the shock he took the minister to Synod, which is like an internal church court. During the investigation it came out the guy wasn't so much a minister as a high-end con man who had ruined the lives of everyone around him for fun and profit. At the very hour the Synod was deliberating on his punishment, the guy dropped dead, halfway through a game of squash, and the whole affair was swept under the blue Presbyterian rug.

I wasn't sure how to take this. It seemed like proof that God existed, but didn't think much of the Church. I knew how He felt. By the time I joined the Sadler crew I had come to think of Jesus as a metaphor. This didn't make Jesus any less real to me, but the Sadlers insisted he wasn't really real unless he was an actual guy with a beard and sandals. I understood their reluctance. In the modern world, the metaphor is a second-class citizen.

By now the winter had settled in like an old dog chewing a soup bone. My days were spent surfing an aluminum ladder above crush rock with a thirty-pound hydraulic nail gun in each hand, slamming them into a slippery plywood wall while the heavens sent buckets of icy water down my sleeves into my armpits. The biggest hazard was a little number called the west coast jig, which is what Harold called it when someone plugged in your power tool while you were standing in a puddle of water.

It was a hard life at the crab dock. I got up before dawn, took Pasheabel to her friend Caitlin's house, then slouched through the rain to the construction site with my tool belt over my shoulder. Of course, winter has always been a war out here. The first white man to winter in these parts was Captain Cook's assistant surgeon, John McKay, who spent Christmas of 1786 with the Nuu-chah-nulth up in Nootka. A week after his ship sailed he broke a taboo and was obliged to spend the rainy season naked under a tree, begging for food. My first winter on the *Loch Ryan* looked like it was going to be on a par.

The Nuu-chah-nulth word for January is *wiyaquam* — "no food getting for a long time." Christian work ethic notwithstanding, even the Sadlers took it easy when the rains came. Work tapered off, and so did the money. Paradoxically, the bills kept rolling in as steady as summer fog. October's moorage came due just as my battery died. A new one would cost $300, but it ran the bilge pump. I had to choose between staying afloat financially or physically. Soon, whenever I saw Art Clarke, I ran. After a week of this I was so embarrassed I had to get off the crab dock, so I chugged over to Jensen's dock to check out the situation there.

Jensen's dock was a sombre spot at the end of Wingen's Lane, in the shadow of the abandoned BC Packers building. As I crouched on the end of the float, staring across the gray water, a shaggy head was thrust from one of the boat hatches. It was Whiskey, my old neighbour, a Tough City original. He grew up at his dad's sawmill out on Grice Bay. One afternoon they were milling a cedar snag from the mountain behind Opitsaht when the blade shattered on a cannonball that had been there since Admiral Gray shelled the place in 1785. Whiskey used the lumber to build a house on the inlet, just across the highway from where my trail led up to the pyramid. One winter his wife left with the kids, and the place devolved into a bachelor paradise. He had his drum kit set up in the living room and an extra fridge just for beer.

Whiskey knew stuff. When I cracked a tooth, it was he who told me to run a Q-Tip along the back of a slug and rub the slime on my gum, which numbed the pain instantly. When a bear broke into the pyramid and ate a ten-pound bag of espresso beans, then washed them down with a gallon of extra-virgin olive oil, it was Whiskey who suggested I replace my door with a floor hatch. He said bears didn't like to dislodge things over their heads. Perhaps this was because the Nuu-chah-nulth have been trapping them for millennia with a setup that drops rocks on them when they dislodge a pole. Days after I finished the hatch I heard the bear coming through the forest like a drunken linebacker. As Whiskey had predicted, my new hatch bewildered the creature. Pasheabel and I lay upstairs, peeking down from the third-floor hatch, quiet as ghosts. We could see the new hatch wobble as the bear jiggled it. After ten minutes it took a break. Then it came back and jiggled the hatch some more. Then it left and never came back. Later I ran into Whiskey at the liquor store. I thanked him, and he introduced me to his new girlfriend. "We're getting hitched."

They fixed up his house as a B&B. They seemed happy, but every night on my way up to the pyramid I heard them going at each other like kestrels. One night she attacked him with a knife, or he attacked her, or they attacked each other. The police came, she got a restraining order, and by spring the B&B was open for business, but Whiskey couldn't go within a hundred metres of the place. Now he was living in the bilge of an old fish boat with a Texas mickey of rye and a loaf of Wonder Bread.

He gave me the scoop on Jensen's dock, which wasn't good: no electricity and very little sun. Anyway, he said, the moorage on all these government docks was the same. If I wanted a break on rent I would have to tie up at the aptly named hurricane buoys, smack in the middle of Father Charles Channel, where the southeasterly hits the water all winter. It looked like I was stuck with steady moorage payments.

I was broke and on the lam from Art, but how wonderful it seemed that I could get warm and dry just by twisting a dial. I had forgotten how easy life is when you don't have wood heat. Firewood had become a real problem in the Sound. The winter before I almost landed in jail just trying to keep my woodshed full.

It all started innocently enough. My friend Stu had spied a giant spruce with the root still on, floating past his house in Warn Bay, which lies across Fortune Channel from the old sawmill at Mosquito Cove. Once there was a gold mine in Warn, but it shut down in 1929, the last inhabitants an old Chinese cook and his run of chickens. Stu lived in a cabin near the mouth of the bay.

When he saw that giant spruce drifting past he came and got me, because the tree was immense and my chainsaw had a three-foot bar. We rode out on Chris's herring skiff. The tree was seven feet across the butt and sixty clear to the first knot. When I looked at all that number-one lumber I knew in my heart we should really mill it into boards. It was worth thousands. But right now I needed firewood, not money. It was only January and I was down to my last cord of hemlock.

I had just started to buck the behemoth into the skiff when an old logger came roaring round the point in the MacBlo launch *Tranquil One*. He was none too tranquil. "You're in trouble now, lads!" he yelled. He claimed some old miner who lived in the next cove had already salvaged the log and planned to mill it into lumber. We just laughed. We knew no one lived in the next cove, the log hadn't been marked or tied off, and Stu had watched it wash up on shore with his own eyes. The truth was, that old logger wanted the tree for himself and was trying to scare us off. He thought we were just some stupid hippie kids. It rankled. Halfway through his speech I gunned my saw and drowned him out. He yelled, "Okay then! I'll tell the cops!"

Back in town the new cop waited for us at Fourth Street dock. We didn't even know until the next day, because we came ashore at the old boat ramp on Grice Bay. I felt pretty smug about slipping the dragnet, but it turned out that old logger was right — we were stupid hippie kids. That log wasn't spruce, it was balsam fir. It went up the chimney as fast as I could load the stove, like I was burning boxes and boxes of Kleenex.

That first winter on the *Loch Ryan* it seemed like sheer decadence to come home soaking and get warm and dry in ten minutes by just lying on the bunk. I delved into a big thick biography of Joseph Campbell called *A Fire In the Mind*. I was surprised to find he had quit school halfway through university and moved off the Grid into the forest, where he lived in a cabin with a crateful of books and a crazy landlord who refused to install running water because he didn't like the class of people it attracted. In 1920 he set out for the west coast, where he became roommates with John Steinbeck. In the summer of 1923 he headed up the California coast in an old fish boat, the *Grampus*. That chapter of the book was called "The *Grampus* Adventure". Under the title was a quote from Steinbeck: "Men need sea-monsters in their personal oceans . . . An ocean without its unnamed monsters would be like a completely dreamless sleep."

The passage reminded me of a time when I was around table-height and found an old toy in the jumble under my bed. It was a set of wooden blocks that fit together to form six different scenes from the Brothers Grimm. I hadn't played with the blocks for years because they weren't much of a challenge. But the illustrations were beautiful. I wanted to see them again.

I spilled the blocks onto the carpet and married two halves of a thundercloud. A third block showed a distant ocean horizon. I thought, Which scene is this? Not *Jack and the Beanstalk*. Not *Goldilocks*. How curious. I had fitted the blocks together a hundred times. I knew each scene by heart. But this wide ocean, this unfamiliar sky . . .

An electric thrill ran through me. I knew it was impossible that the blocks contained an unknown scene. But as each piece fit I was faced with the fact that I had never seen this seascape before. Then the last few blocks slid into place and I realized what had happened. It was the scene of the fearsome sea monster. I was unfamiliar with the image because when I was little I had been too afraid to put it together. The sea monster had red coals for eyes, and their glow had terrified me. I dreamed I became a man and forgot the fearsome serpent was real and went swimming in Loch Ness. Later my parents wept as the sinister bachelor on *The News At Ten* said, "He vanished without trace."

I longed to go back to that moment when I thought there was an unknown image in the jumble of blocks. For a spell, the impossible had been real. But when I became a man I put away childish things. At least, that's the theory. One summer I was trolling for sockeye off Nootka, running down the coast at eight knots through a summer fog. The skipper stood in the wheelhouse door and told me in terse, cigarette-punctured prose that he had lost four friends along this shore. "They found nothing. Just a gumboot."

He went inside and drowsed over the wheel, and I stood alone in the cockpit for hours, cutting the day's catch. Dark sky, diesel roar, the itch of salmon blood under my thumbnail. Grab, slash, grab, slash. Around one in the morning I still had a tote of pink salmon to cut. They were worth almost nothing. I threw one into the churning wake. Behind me I heard a blast of air, like a whale.

I turned and squinted into the dark. I tossed another salmon. I saw a curve of shadow, then a second wake appeared beside the boat's. Whatever was back there must be huge. Exhaustion had stripped my mind down to the wiring, but I had to know what it was. I clambered onto the gurdy. My boots felt slippery on the brass wheels. I twisted the cockpit light around so that it shone behind the boat. Now I could see a huge bronze shape undulating beneath the waves. It wasn't a whale. Whales don't have wings. This creature had great golden wings, thirty feet from tip to tip, and I could see every feather. For that dark shining moment, sea monsters were real. I threw another salmon, and the creature rose up through the surface with an enormous *whoosh!* Its great jaws snapped shut on the fish. The golden wings were gone.

It was a sea lion. A big old bull. He bobbed in the water and stared at me, his mouth pink as bubble gum, his eyes green as glass floats in the cockpit light. He dived under the wake and the wings reappeared. The golden feathers were just phosphorescent bubbles streaming from the tips of his flippers.

It was the death of God, that moment, when the jumble of magical blocks clicked into place and the world made sense once more. Just a sea lion, miles out on the workaday ocean, staring into my eyes, looking for more free fish.

That moment was why I feared the Grid, and modern life in general. I saw such things as the end of mystery and the beginning of survival. That was why I had run into so many rocks trying to fathom the *Loch Ryan*'s engine. I secretly wanted engines to make no sense, to keep the mystery swimming through the blocks alive. But I had confused the depths of my soul with the depths of the sea. There was the real ocean, with its real creatures, and there was Steinbeck's "personal ocean", with its monsters. I wanted the best of both worlds: a real ocean to sail, and a personal ocean with monsters to battle.

Mixing concrete with metaphors is a common mistake. Like those poor alchemists, who spent their lives trying to transform lead into gold, unaware that the process was just a metaphor for enlightenment. Or Fred Tibbs, who sought transformation into beauty, but confused his face with an island. Or the Sadlers, who knew Jesus was real because they felt him in their hearts, but mistook the feeling for a carpenter from desert lands.

That night I read "The *Grampus* Adventure" with fascination. Campbell, Steinbeck and Ed Ricketts motored up the coast all the way to Alaska. It was an American book, so there was a blank on the map between Seattle and Anchorage. But it seemed likely that Ed had taken the boat up the outside of Vancouver Island via his old stomping grounds at the hotel on Stubbs. I had pictured Campbell as a heroic character from some distant time and place. But now it looked like he had once dropped anchor within sight of where I was moored. Again I sensed that mysterious membrane that connects every human life, even mine and Joseph Campbell's.

In the belly of that winter I glimpsed that the monsters of the real ocean were personal, and the monsters of the personal ocean were real. It might be possible to have the best of both worlds if I kept them separate and paid each its due.

As the days dawned earlier and brighter I delved to the bottom of the bilge, into places I had feared to go in case I killed the mystery of the thing. The hull under the engine had been coated with a mixture of piling tar, creosote, and recycled engine oil. Art's brother, Huey Clarke, had invented the stuff at his boat shed up in Ahousaht. It seemed old Sammy had been liberal in its application.

"Oh yes," said Art. "Creosote was Sammy's religion. Every Sunday morning he was down in the bilge with a brush."

I had gone up to the shed to apologize for my moorage tardiness. Art said not to worry, just so long as I paid up. "Anyway, I lose track sometimes."

It was no wonder the hull had stayed free of rot all those years. Huey's mixture had pickled the wood. It was amazing stuff, but I didn't want it for a roommate. I scraped it off pound by pound, and when I got to the very bottom of the bilge I found forty lead bars buried in the toxic sludge. I stacked the bars on deck and cleaned them off with gasoline. Art came walking down the fifth finger with his kid and a couple of fishing rods. "Hey, Art," I said, "look what I found in the bilge."

"That's your ballast. Hang onto that. It's worth a dollar a pound."

I hauled a bar up to the big red clam scale and weighed it. Eighty pounds. Times forty bars. At a dollar a pound they were worth three grand, exactly what I paid for the boat. Lead into gold.

SIX

"THERE'S A SANDBAR DEAD AHEAD!" SOPHIE
yelled down from the wheelhouse roof. I looked at the chart
and realized I had no idea where we were. We had motored
up to the mouth of Indian River to visit Jim at Gunner
Inlet, and now we were lost in a maze of shallow channels at
the end of Grice Bay. I had been here only once before, at
low low tide in the middle of the night. I came with Crabber
Dave to dig horse clams for bait. It was a cold, uncanny
landscape of silt and eelgrass, with siphon squirts from the
clams glinting in the lantern's beam. Not a good place to run
aground.

I throttled back, but we came within thirty feet of the
sandbar. The tide was falling and there was little chance we'd
have made it off again. I had been with Sophie for less than a
week and she'd saved my ass twice.

The first time was when I careened the hull and replaced
the zincs. The job had to be done every summer just after
the mussels bloomed, otherwise they'd be eating into the
hull all year. I motored up to the grid in the dead of night. It
was my third time, and I was getting cocky. I swung the
stern round too far, the prop hit a rock and the engine died
with a bang. Sophie was still awake because she had been
partying with the pirates on the *Oldfield*. She helped me

manoeuvre the boat over the beams just as the keel scraped bottom. A few minutes later the *Loch Ryan* would have been at the mercy of gravity as the tide dropped.

I sat on the dock, shaking. Sophie said in a thick French accent, "I 'ad a dream about you." In her dream we were flying together into a giant mandala of pure love. It sounded good. We walked over to her boat, *Ariene,* one of the new flotilla of retired trollers that had arrived on the dock that summer in the wake of the Mifflin Plan. Most of the new-comers brought drums and canines, and Art was going nuts trying to keep the dog shit off the floats. But Sophie was a steady sort. She had painted the *Ariene*'s hull a light gold colour, oiled the mahogany window frames and hung little lace curtains inside. Then she painted the trim an outra-geous shade of magenta. The combination was unexpect-edly beautiful, and so was she. Beauty is sometimes just an accident of bone and skin, but her use of colour really caught my eye.

We lay in the fo'c's'le bunk and she told me she had wanted to join the circus and dangle by her long black hair, twirling like a sycamore seed above the ring of sand. She settled for life as a dancer, which had been good, but now she was thirty. Time for a change.

She handled the pirates on the *Oldfield* like they were boy scouts, and she was good under pressure. When we got lost on the way to Gunner Inlet she sat calmly on the wheel-house roof and rapped whenever I came close to running aground. Eventually I looked at the chart and realized I had confused Indian Island with Warne Island. I brought the boat round and ran back through a bay so shallow the eel-grass rustled along the rolling chocks. At the end of the bay I found a deep green channel and ran up the side of Indian Island towards Gunner.

There are three principal winds in the Clayoquot. The southeast blows warm and damp, the northwest blows clear and cold, and in midsummer the westerly blows warm and sunny, which is why the local newspaper is called the *Westerly News*. That day the westerly blasted up the inlet, and the entrance to Gunner was choppy with whitecaps. We had to row in on my new runabout.

Jim's cabin squatted in a pocket of dappled sunlight, above a meadow that was the bootprint of an old homestead. Ralph Tieleman's black fish boat lay rotting on the grass. Jim poured some kind of hippie zinger tea. Sun and wind blew through the leaves. Rusted light and shadows rushed through the room. Sophie threw her clothes in a pile and didn't touch them until the end of the day. She dived into the bay and swam until all we could see was the tattooed serpent that coiled around her bum.

"She's a keeper," said Jim. "Where did you get the little runabout?"

I had seen her tipped against the wall of Rollie Arnet's boat shed, an old red building that stuck out over the water on pilings, chock to the rafters with wooden blocks, furled sails and miles upon miles of rope and chain. The runabout was ancient and half her ribs were rotten, but something about the shape of the caravel hull attracted me. She was just the right size for the *Loch Ryan*. With such a runabout I could go ashore in places where there was no dock, like Hippie Beach.

Rollie didn't want to sell until I mentioned I had bought the *Loch Ryan,* at which point he gave me the runabout for fifty bucks. "The *Loch Ryan* was Harold Arnet's boat," he said. Harold had been Rollie's dad's cousin. It turned out Sam Eadie had bought the *Loch Ryan* from one generation of Arnets and sold her to the next. His whole fishing career had been the filling in an Arnet sandwich. That's not as unlikely a coincidence as it seems. The Arnets are Tofino's first family of fishing. Once there were so many Arnets in town that people started calling it Arnetville, until the Feds reminded everyone that the place was named after Vincente Tofino, a Spanish hydrographer who had never even been here. Nowadays you have to go to the graveyard if you want to be surrounded by Arnets. These things go in waves.

The Arnet saga began in 1898, when a Vancouver fish packing company sent Jakob Arnet up from Vancouver to find out if there were enough salmon in the Clayoquot to warrant a cannery. Jakob liked it so much he stayed for five generations. His name is on the very first fishing licence issued for the Sound. In George Nicholson's book, *Vancouver Island's West Coast,* there is a photograph of Jakob's daughter, Alma, and his six sons, all fishermen. Four of them wear Navy uniforms. Harold is the handsome one with curly hair. He fished the *Loch Ryan* from just after the War until he became the federal Fisheries officer in 1954. To his left in the photo is brother Edgar, who almost didn't make it into the picture, thanks to an incident up north.

The year was 1920. Edgar went fishing for halibut off Kodiak Island, plugged the hold and headed back across open ocean to Anchorage. Halfway there a pin sheared, the propellor fell off and sank to the bottom of the Bering Strait, and they found themselves a thousand miles out with no radio. It looked like certain death.

Edgar had been fishing with a sail rigged on a boom to keep the boat steady while they were hauling in the net. Now he dismantled the boom and ran it sideways across the gunnels. The crew carved a hole in a hardwood block, packed it with halibut grease and ran the boom through it. They carved slots in the ends of the boom and stuck pen-boards from the hold into the slots so that the boat looked like the skeleton of a paddle wheeler. Edgar ran a chain around the boom and down to a deck winch that ran off the engine. When he gunned the motor the chain turned the boom, the pen-board paddles slapped into the water, and they were underway again.

The paddle blades kept snapping, and the crew had to whittle fast to keep the contraption in spare parts. Eight days later, and almost out of wood, the boys spotted the white peaks of Alaska on the horizon. An American steamer running down the coast saw they were in trouble and towed them in to Anchorage. Edgar sold the catch, fixed the prop and headed straight back out for more.

I figured if Edgar could pull off a stunt like that, I could get Rollie's runabout shipshape. Perhaps I could steam some strips of oak in a metal pipe, Wingen-style, and sister the damaged ribs. But when I took a closer look I saw that some-one had already done that. Every second rib was good. I tore out the older set and she was fine. I stripped her down to the planks, replaced the rotten transom and put in a bunghole. I remounted the *Loch Ryan*'s trolling davits so they stuck out over the transom and hung the runabout from them on blocks. Halfway through all this, Sophie asked if I wanted a girlfriend or a boat. I hesitated, and that was enough to spark a fight. The truth is, I just wasn't sure. We agreed to spend the weekend together and talk things through.

But on Friday afternoon I got back from the Sadler show to find a big old refrigerator lying on my transom deck. For an hour I was bemused. Then I remembered that Peter Buckland had asked if I could bring his new fridge up to Hesquiat, where he had taken over Cougar Annie's home-stead in Boat Basin.

I motored up the coast. It was a sunny afternoon, and I

felt an inexplicable thrill when I ran full throttle towards the open horizon north of Hot Springs Cove. Up ahead lay the place where the *mamaalthi* first met the Nuu-chah-nulth. In history books it's James Cook who made contact, when he went ashore at Nootka. But four years earlier the Spanish schooner *Santiago* anchored off Matlahaw Point and traded with the Hesquiahts, who paddled out in their canoes. Cook got the nod because the Spaniards didn't come ashore, and this has always confused the Nuu-chah-nulth, who don't make such distinctions. For them the important part was the verb of contact, not the noun of *terra firma*.

When I saw Hesquiat up ahead I felt a thrill of fear. Many good ships had come to grief in these waters. Old Joe MacLeod's troller *Muns* lay high on the sand at Matlahaw Point, with a square hole cut through her ribs where they salvaged the engine. Even big ocean-going vessels like the three-hundred-foot freighter *Tahsis Princess* had met disaster on the treacherous boulders strewn around Hesquiat Point.

I heard the story of the *Princess* from the latter-day Spanish explorer Henry Nolla, who lived in a handmade A-frame at the south end of Chestermans Beach. My first job in town was babysitting his daughter Nuri while her mom went to work in the clinic up at Ahousaht. Life at the A-frame was simple. Water came from a red-handled pump in the kitchen, money from selling carved masks and bowls. Henry looked like Father Time in a Blake engraving and never wore clothes unless he had to go to town. Nor did the young women who came to whittle cedar and sunbathe between the driftwood logs around the carving shed.

Like a lot of people, Henry moved to Clayoquot by mistake. In 1959 he set out from Spain to see the jungles of South America. His sister ran the Chilean consulate in Stockholm. She said she could get him a work visa, so he travelled north to Sweden. Months passed, and still no paperwork. One day there was a lineup outside the Canadian consulate next door. He asked what was going on.

"They're *giving away* Canadian work visas!"

He figured Canada was closer to South America than Sweden was. Two weeks later he was working in the mine at Uranium City. But not long after he arrived the whole place shut down, leaving miles of schools and malls and suburbs that slowly returned to the muskeg. As compensation, the company offered him a job welding at the Draw Creek iron mine above Kennedy Lake. He figured British Columbia was closer to South America than Uranium City was. Perhaps he could work his way down the coast.

There were fourteen welders at the Draw Creek mine, and the other thirteen were from Oakalla prison. In those days the Feds had a program that was supposed to get junkie loggers off heroin by farming them out to isolated logging camps and mines, away from the Downtown Eastside and its plentiful supply of smack. Plans like that only make sense if you've never worked in the bush. Main and Hastings pales compared to what goes down in the woods on a Saturday night.

Henry had never welded before, but the rest of the Draw Creek crew had the shakes so bad he was the only one who could draw a straight bead. Bob Wingen came out looking for a welder for the shipyard and took him back to Tough City. He never made it to South America. There was too much fun to be had right here in the Clayoquot, helping Whitey and Neil Botting pit-lamp deer from the deck of Bob's motor launch.

When the *Tahsis Princess* ran aground at Hesquiat in 1967, the owners flew Henry, Bob, Whitey, Neil and the rest of the Clayoquot pirates up to Boat Basin to see what they could salvage. The ship was insured with Lloyd's of London. There was so much money at stake that the men were forbidden contact with the outside world. Their wives didn't even get a phone call to tell them they were still alive, although that was nothing new.

The *Princess* lay on her port side, taking a thousand gallons an hour through a gash below the waterline. The plan was to salvage what they could before the rising tide rolled her into the deep. But when Bob checked the engine there was just enough compression to turn the flywheel over once. They might be able to save her. He rattled off a telegram to Lloyd's and sat tight.

The tide began to flood. Whitey kept the water level down with a bilge pump made from an old Volvo engine, but the cargo of oranges, toilet paper and margarine kept clogging up the works. Henry had to dive into that mush hour after hour to clear the intake valve. He got stickier and stickier until he couldn't stand it any more. He swam under the hull, which lay almost flat along the bottom, forming a V so tight he had to take off his tanks and drag them along beside him. His only light was a twelve-volt bulb sealed with candle wax to the end of an orange Co-op extension cord. He found the breach and they patched it with a mixture of galley towels and cement.

Around sunset, Bob checked the tide tables and realized tonight was the highest tide of the year. If they were going to rescue the *Princess,* they had to do it now. Lloyd's still hadn't replied to his cable. He gathered the men and told them they could probably get the ship off the rocks and run her straight up onto the sand in front of Hesquiat. If the boat went down they might be liable. But if they got her to shore they might have salvage rights worth millions.

Almost high tide, and still no word from London. Finally

Bob said, "God hates a coward," and called in Barry Grum-bach's dad, Ray, on the *Gyppo 5*. As the sea rose the *Gyppo 5* strained to keep the freighter upright. Bob gave the signal and Henry got clear of the bilge pump. Sandy Bradshaw ran the length of the cavernous engine room, firing blasts of ether into the giant blowers. Neil Botting hit the ignition, the massive flywheel clunked over once and stopped, then the cylinders roared to life. The *Princess* came off the rocks at a forty-five degree angle and stayed that way because a load of tractor parts had settled halfway up the side of the hold. Neil hung on to the wheel, and the great ship thundered towards the sand and up onto the beach. When the tide ebbed she was high and dry. Saved.

The owners were horrified. They had been anticipating a big fat cheque from Lloyd's. Now these Clayoquot pirates had queered the deal, with salvage rights to boot. Lloyd's, so mysteriously silent while Bob had risked disaster, flew a man up to Hesquiat first thing Monday morning. Within hours the crew was welcoming him aboard, which they shouldn't have done. The moment his foot touched the deck he reclaimed the vessel. From a legal standpoint, Bob was still under contract. What he'd been up to on the weekend was not the company's concern. The *Tahsis Princess* made it to Vancouver under her own power, where the owners argued with Lloyd's for a year until she sank tied to the dock. The pirates got paid only for their time.

Now I had almost reached Hesquiat, and it didn't look good. Whitecaps crossed the bay. I brought the *Loch Ryan* closer to the shore, but the westerly had picked up. Waves redounded off the cliffs and the boat began to yaw. I heard a crashing noise, and when I looked outside I saw Peter's refrigerator slamming back and forth across the deck like a shuttle in a loom. Just shy of Boulder Point my nerve failed and I ran for home. When I got back to the dock it was Saturday around noon. Sophie was steamed. She had been waiting for hours. I had forgotten all about our plans.

Suddenly, working on my engine seemed much simpler than working on a relationship. Engines were predictable, whereas women were an unfathomable mystery. I had raised Pasheabel from an egg, and still I had no grasp of the female mind. Sometimes Sophie and I seemed to be on the same page, but mostly we were different as nouns and verbs. No wonder couples don't see eye to eye on their most basic needs, like love and money. The winter I spent with River at the Pyramid we had so little money we could barely afford organic veggies. Then one night I got home from the fish plant to find River close to tears of happiness. She had found a way to parlay our last two hundred bucks into fifty grand, which she would then use to overthrow the patriarchy. How? She pulled out a crumpled photocopy . . .

"Women Helping Women" was obviously the Pyramid of Women, which I had thought was lost to memory. But here it was again, with a newly sprouted mission statement that solemnly bonded River to give half of her windfall to women's shelters, rainforest coalitions and so forth. This was music to her ears, because she lived to give. I thought she would be grateful if I saved her from the scam. I showed her the math. I slept on the couch. And now that I lived on a boat, I didn't even have a couch.

Sophie and I fought into the evening, then I got drunk with Shorty while he tried to explain how I could build an on-demand pump for my shower. He showed me his, which he had made from scratch. I couldn't even understand how it worked. I knew just looking at the little mechanism that I would always be second-rate at this stuff. I could spend my life fixing up the *Loch Ryan,* but I would never have the mechanical genius of guys like Shorty and Bob Wingen. My calling was art.

Shorty was just the opposite — a practical man who wanted to be an artist. He loved art. He had all sorts of paintings and carvings by local artists stuffed into his boat. Over the bunk was a giant skull that Godfrey had carved from a solid block of cedar. Rumour had it the skull was worth thousands, but Shorty wouldn't sell. His newest acquisition was a portrait of Sophie that Godfrey had sketched onto a cedar plank while they drank rum together. He had really caught her strange beauty in his delicious lines. "She's something," said Shorty. "She's been through everything, that one. She's seen it all."

As I staggered back to the *Loch Ryan,* Chris from the *Old-field* came weaving down the dock in the opposite direction with a frozen albacore in each fist, arms held wide like stabilizer poles. He was just back from tuna fishing. He gave me one of the tunas and we drank a nightcap on the *Oldfield.* He threw a postcard down on the galley table.

"Got one of these?"

It was an invitation to Wayne and Cathy's wedding. Those two were a typical Clayoquot couple. She was a dancer and he was an ivory merchant. He didn't murder elephants, but he had a licence to trade fossilized walrus tusks and narwhal horns. When he got a choice chunk he would carve it into a sculpture with a set of old dentist tools and sell it to a newspaper baron back east. Now he and Cathy planned to marry on summer solstice, up at his float house in Freedom Cove.

When the big day came, Eric Vezina knocked on my wheelhouse door. Eric was a handsome young Québecois who sang like Sting and could split a round of wood even when it was one big knot. His only failing was that he never listened. When you talked to him, his eyes would glaze over and you knew he hadn't heard a word you'd said, he was already thinking of what he was going to say next. The habit infuriated me because I did it too. Our conversations sometimes bordered on ridiculous.

Eric grew up in northern Quebec, enduring winters so bitterly cold that when the wind blew he could hear the nails in the house frame cracking like knuckles. He was amazed to find a patch of Canada where you could survive the winter in a tent if need be. He bought a sailboat and tried to fix her up, but she was a money pit. She ended her days with a one-way ticket to the glory hole behind Vargas and a midnight shotgun blast through the hull. Down she went. Now he needed a ride to the wedding.

Freedom Cove lay round the back of Meares just past Quait Bay, so we stopped in to visit Gord and Erin. Gord laughed with glee when he saw how trim the *Loch Ryan* looked, but I barely recognized the Floatel. The owner had flown in for the day and didn't like the new decor. He bought a hundred-year-old barn in Abbotsford, took it apart nail by nail and used the worn, wormy wood to re-cover the walls we had painstakingly painted. The only trace of our hard work was the cupboard under the stairs.

We ran down the coast to Freedom Cove. The entrance was narrow and rocky, but these days I had no fear. I waved away the pilot boat. So many boats were packed into the cove that you could walk right across it without wetting your feet. Every pirate, freebooter and freeloader in the Clayoquot was there. People were drinking homemade beer, eating giant hash brownies, jumping from the rigging and landing on guitars and deck chairs and in the water. I myself did not spare the mead. There were six fifties folded into the nook beside the compass. It was my final payment on the *Loch Ryan*. Monday morning, after a quick trip to the bank, I would be home-free. Scot-free. Free Willy-free.

At dusk the bigger boats began to leave. Freedom Cove was only three feet deep at low tide, and already the entrance was studded with boulders. Chris, fully lubed, fired up the *Oldfield* and she bellowed into the sunset like a wounded beast. Nigel from the liquor store asked me to lead Chris out through the rocks. By the time I got the *Loch Ryan* untied, Chris was backing up at top speed so he could make the turnaround. Harvey, passed out on his bunk in the *Norvag,* heard the noise and peered out his porthole just in time to see the *Oldfield*'s huge Tremclad ass swing past, inches from his hull. She thundered down the narrow channel like a shopping granny shouldering her way to a bargain bin, and I followed timidly in her wake until we reached the deep waters around Mussel Rock.

Some memories are so clear the cops will be able to fish them out of my wallet once I'm dead. In this one the *Oldfield* is outlined against the crimson sky, and Chris, cut from black cardboard, kicks the anchor off the prow in a drunken Cossack jig, arms folded, two steps forward, two steps back and — *kick!*

The anchor smashed the water like a hammer through a mirror. That anchor was huge. It made my anchor look like it was embroidered on a hat. Instead of dropping my own I tied up to the *Oldfield* and passed out on my bunk. Next morning I woke to the trundle of the *Oldfield*'s anchor chain. All that came up was the rotted end of the cable. We had been adrift all night. I might just as easily have woken on the rocks with the fifties for my final payment bobbing beside me.

I should have gone straight home to the dock and sat there shaking, but that's not the pirate lifestyle. I decided to head north round the top of Meares and visit Stu at Warn

Bay. Eric whipped up a liquid breakfast and we motored off through Matlset Narrows.

We sighted Warn Bay within the hour. Stu's place was in a nook just beyond the entrance. From the north it was hidden by trees, and I ran right past it. I didn't realize until I looked back and saw the cabin roof. I said to Eric, "Missed it." He nodded. But when I brought the boat around he asked what I was doing. "I thought we were going to visit Stu?"

He hadn't even listened. I explained the whole thing again, and he nodded, but his eyes were already glazed, like he was thinking about snow tires. Suddenly he cut me off and pointed. "Look! Look! There's Stu's place! You went right past it!"

It was like talking to the side of a boat. I got so pissed off I whacked the side of his head. He turned to me with murder in his eyes. There was a crash like a cannon puking and the *Loch Ryan* keeled over onto her starboard side. I had run right up onto the rocks. Eric screamed for a life jacket, even though technically we were ashore. I clung to the wheel, slammed the engine into reverse and gunned it. The prop washed just enough water under the hull to float her off the rocks, and we slid backwards into the channel. When I looked behind me water was gushing up from the belly of the boat into the hold. We must have popped a plank. The *Loch Ryan* was going down and nothing could save her.

But it was only the bilge water, knocked up into the stern, and now pouring back over the rear bulkhead like a tiny gray Niagara. Moments later we were motoring down the channel again, still in one piece. I told Eric to take the wheel, then I went outside and projectile-vomited over the transom.

By the time I reached Fourth Street dock that mysterious connective membrane had struck again. The story was all over town. Some wag had already spoonerized *Loch Ryan* into *Rock Lyin'*. I sat on the dock, shaking. "Don't worry about it," said Chris. "Never been aground? Never been around."

But I began to fear that I had mixed the metaphor of pirate freedom with the concrete of my daily life. I wanted the best of both worlds, and to do that I had to keep them separate. Freedom in the mind, responsibility at the wheel. I decided to quit drinking and smoking pot to see if it would reduce my confusion. But just like a boat, life has its own momentum. As soon as I tried to make that turnaround I felt a pull in the opposite direction. Within a week I got a call from a friend down in Ucluelet.

Tofino and Ucluelet are like twins. Tough City stands at the mouth of Clayoquot Sound, and twenty miles south, Ucluelet guards the entrance to Barkley Sound, although some said Ukee was more like a bouncer than a guard. I didn't buy into the anti-Ukee sentiment because I had noticed anything that happened in one town was reflected in the other. In our town, Whiskey's girlfriend got a restraining order on him. Meanwhile, down in Ukee, Whiskey's brother Des got a restraining order on *his* girlfriend because she cut down the welcome sign outside his Big Woody Trailer Park with a chainsaw. Ukee had logged the mountain behind them, while we had left ours untouched. During the War all Japanese property in Tofino was seized and divvied up, but in Ucluelet the land was set aside until the dispossessed returned. There was even a funhouse mirror version of myself — Chris Bennett. He surfed, wrote books and had just bought an old east coast lobster boat named the *Scotia Queen*.

People took us for brothers, which was fine by me because we saw eye to eye on everything except the Tree of Life in the Garden of Eden. Chris thought it was a marijuana plant, and I thought it was a metaphor. He wrote a book called *Green Gold,* with masses of quotes and photographs of Babylonian temple friezes to prove his point, but I still didn't buy it. Pot seemed like a poor candidate for the Old Testament drug of choice, although the visuals are hilarious. Picture Moses waffling between munchies and paranoia as he forbids the Israelites to gather manna on the Sabbath. Now Chris had written a second book, *Sex, Drugs, Violence and the Bible,* and he wanted me to do a painting for the cover.

I hitched down to Ukee and found the *Scotia Queen* moored at the end of the government dock. The boat next to her had sunk in her moorings. From the depths her blank wheelhouse windows stared up at me like the eye sockets of a skull. The idea of the *Loch Ryan* ending up like that, with dim shapes flitting through the fo'c's'le, horrified me. It was like seeing the soul of someone who has gone mad.

The *Scotia Queen* was a lot further along than the *Loch Ryan.* The hold was already closed in and the wheelhouse was big and roomy. Chris showed me his book manuscript on a twelve-volt laptop and described what he wanted for the cover. I begged off because my heart wasn't in it. He offered me a bowl of bud. I said I had quit. He promised me his beautiful Becker longboard. I said I hadn't been surfing in months. He rummaged through the hold and pulled out all sorts of old brass fittings, chains and gears. I needed that stuff. Once my cabin was extended over the fish hold it would be impossible to dock solo from the wheelhouse. I would have to extend the chain drive back to the cockpit so I could steer from there. To do that I needed the gear Chris had laid before me. We shook. To seal the deal we shared a bowl of bud. Half an hour later I was so high I thought the *Scotia Queen* was sloping, and I had to cling to the wheelhouse floor.

A week later, still mad at myself for caving so quickly, I motored over to Stone Island to visit Sam from the Floatel crew. Sam showed me a magic mushroom that had grown on a stump outside. It was the size of my fist. Was there no escape from the drugs in this town?

We drank coffee on his sundeck and looked across the channel at Tough City while Pasheabel's little dog, Zeus, ran up and down the planks, shaking a white sponge like it was a rat. From town, Sam's place seemed to lie in the heart of paradise, surrounded by great walls of trees and backed by the distant snowy peaks of Strathcona Park. But from his deck all we could see was town, which that morning looked like an industrial park with a mohawk. "That's a funny place to build," he said. "It faces north, it's always dark, it — holy crap! What's this?"

It was a chunk of white fleshy material. There were other chunks all over the deck. Zeus stopped worrying her white sponge and looked up at us guiltily. It wasn't a white sponge. It was the mushroom. A magic mushroom bigger than her head. I said, "I think we should go for a walk."

Zeus ran up and down the beach, crouched, took a shit, buried it, lay down, leaped up, trampled imaginary rushes into a bed and tried to climb up my leg, all at the same time. Her eyes looked like teacups, then like saucers, then like flying saucers. Her fluffy white coat dampened until the skin showed dark underneath. At one point it seemed like she was trying to talk. I was terrified her little heart would burst. How would I explain that to Pasheabel?

Finally the stone broke like a fever and she fell asleep on my lap, kick-starting the tiny phantom motorbike of her dreams. I almost wept with relief. I learned a valuable lesson that day. But Zeus learned nothing. At sunset we walked down to the beach again, and she saw a regular mushroom growing under a log and gobbled it whole.

"I guess she liked it," said Sam.

But I felt like I'd been shown my pirate lifestyle from above. I quit every drug except caffeine that very day.

Remember those færie rings, where a man gets drawn in by the music and dancing, and whirls dervishes round and round, and when he wakes up ten years have whistled past, and he's old? That's what a decade of smoking pot in Tough City looks like from above. Suddenly I made major headway on my cabin extension. Daytime became less dreamlike and my sleep grew thick with dreams, until one night I dreamed I was back in the harbour at Stonehaven. The ocean had rolled back to reveal a desert landscape pocked by ruined derricks and scaffolds that were silhouetted against a yellow sky. For some reason the sun was setting in the east. I stood at the wheel of the *Loch Ryan* and gunned the engine, and we trundled along the top of the great sandstone pier until I felt the keel lift and we began to gain altitude. The wheel felt a little tight, but I didn't care. The *Loch Ryan* could fly! What a boat! I brought her round towards the open horizon and we soared into the great red disc of the sun.

When I woke my chest was filled with hope. The dream seemed connected to Sophie's dream of flying into that giant mandalla of love. Perhaps it was the mental flash I'd been waiting for, an omen that we were destined to be together. When I told Sophie my dream she was furious, because she wasn't even in it. I had flown into the sun with the *Loch Ryan*, not her, so if anything, I was in love with my boat. I mumbled and backtracked, but I knew what she said was true. I had mistaken my boat for a woman.

That evening the dock boomed with hippie drums and didjeridoos, so I ran the *Loch Ryan* five miles out to sea to get some peace. Vancouver Island dwindled to a distant range of mountains that shone like elephant bones in the marmalade light. *Nuu-chah-nulth* — "all along the shining mountains." Gazing at those golden peaks I felt a great swell of compassion for every human soul, trapped in our tiny cells, with our heartbreaking view of eternity. I had wanted to be a typical Clayoquot couple, but it looked like I was destined for a solo career, like old Sam Eadie. It had been easy to follow the song of my soul when it led me towards love. It was not so easy now that it beckoned me into this vast solitude.

But then, it seemed like a miracle that I had ever fallen in love at all. From early on I had myself pegged as a drifter. I still felt filled with hope, and this hope had something to do with the horizon, as if some voice had whispered in my third ear, Who knows what chartless loves might lie in the unknown regions beyond that line? For the first time I had an inkling that there might be life after Clayoquot.

A few weeks later Sophie kissed me goodbye from the back of Shorty's station wagon, and in the Fall we got a postcard from San Diego, where she had hooked up with the skipper of a fifty-foot yacht. Nothing of her remained in Clayoquot Sound, except for her portrait on Shorty's boat, and the name of the *Loch Ryan*'s little runabout, *Sophie*.

SEVEN

"WHAT THE HELL IS THAT? SAID SHORTY. WE were drinking rum on the deck of his boat and watching a mysterious column of water race back and forth in front of Opitsaht. Shorty was celebrating because someone had offered him five grand for Godfrey's skull. "I'll never sell," he said, "but let's celebrate anyway."

The mysterious white column must have been twenty feet high and was moving too fast to be caused by anything human. Waterspout? Sea monster? Suddenly it changed tack and headed straight for us. Moments later, Gilley Palm thundered past the end of the dock in a cigarette boat. Rumour said he'd bought it with an insurance claim from an accident he was partly responsible for. The boat was half the size of a canoe, and its hull was raked at such an angle that we could see Meares Island under the keel. The only part of the boat that was actually in the water was the prop, which was sending up the white arc of spray we'd seen all the way over at Opitsaht.

People said Gilley was no good, but he reminded me of the Blackface dancers, a caste of Clayoquot braves who were formidable in battle but dangerous at a potlach. Once the drums got going they had to be lashed to cedar slabs and hoisted into the longhouse rafters, otherwise they'd kill everybody. Once the *mamaalthi* had a similar setup for handling that kind of energy. On the wall at the Legion there's a roster of thirty names, young men who left this little town for the Great War. A third never returned, and there's a small hand-drawn star beside each name, like the star on the chart beside the dangerous rock at the mouth of Hot Springs Cove. Nowadays these dangerous characters are mixed in with the general population, and it's difficult to distinguish them from those who simply have to be locked away for the public good, unless you watch them growing up.

In the hallway of the school there's a wall of class photos that go back years. Sometimes while I waited for Pasheabel I would pick out people I knew. That girl works in the bank. That guy's in a Mexican jail. Some faces had changed completely with age, but Gilley was no challenge: a sly grin in the back row, a jean jacket and a cowlick, his arm slightly blurred because he was up to something at the moment of the flash.

His dad was Rod Palm, a diver who lived in the old North Vancouver ferry, now dry-docked on Strawberry Island. Shorty and I could see the island from where we sat. Framed by giant cedars, with a line of laundry flapping white in the wind, the old wooden boat made a classic west coast scene — especially now, with Gilley swishing back and forth like an albino rooster right in front of the place, trying to get his old man's goat.

Rod came to the window, watched Gilley for a bit and went back inside. He doesn't fluster easily. One time he dived down to a car that went in the water near William Head prison. When he opened the trunk a giant octopus wrapped its suckered limbs around his head and tried to pull him inside. Rod stuck his respirator into its beak and it let him go. That's called calm under fire, and the apple didn't fall far from the tree. When Gilley was six, Rod fell over the side of a herring skiff, wearing waders that filled and dragged him down. Gilley brought the boat around, got a grip on his dad's suspenders and saved his life. At twelve he was helping Rod dive on a shipwreck they thought might be the legendary *Tonquin,* filling canisters with air from a scuba tank and floating salvaged timbers up to the surface.

Most authorities held that the *Tonquin* foundered up in Nootka after being blown to bits in a fight with the locals in June 1811. But old Edith Simon, who was born on Wickaninnish Island around 1880, remembered it differently. In 1974 she told Rod that the *Tonquin* sank near Tin Wis Beach. In her version the ship wasn't blown to smithereens; she sank slowly after a crippling explosion. Some braves who survived the blast tried to tow her to Echachist, but there was a stiff westerly blowing so they towed her back to Tin Wis. She foundered in the middle of Templar Channel, with the tip of the mainmast sticking out of the water at a rakish angle.

Joe Martin had heard that too, from Albert Charlie. The mast was visible for decades in the bay right between Joe's new house on Echachist and my pyramid. All those years I had been staring at the very spot where the Natives said the good ship lay.

Edith's was an oral history, which most people see as a high-end variation of the party game Telephone, where you whisper a sentence around a room and it changes in a hugely amusing fashion. But oral histories are in fact concise as legal briefs. Edith's account sets the time of year around June by mentioning the westerly, and the location by having the men tow the boat between two points, Echachist and Tin Wis. It's all about the verbs. Everything is recalled through action, which makes a good story, one that will last as long as a well-loved boat. The kicker: Rod noticed there was also a stiff westerly blowing in the *mamaalthi*'s written history.

In that version it was the year before the War of 1812, and the whole continent was strung higher than an Irish setter. Canadian traders backed by British capital had developed a network of contacts with the Natives of the Pacific Northwest. New York financier John Jacob Astor wanted a slice of the pie for America, so he sent the warship *Tonquin* to establish a Yankee trading post at the mouth of the Columbia River.

The *Tonquin* was a fine ship, made four hundred miles a day, and sported twenty cannon breeches. But the crew was all at odds. The captain was a strange and brittle man named Jonathan Thorn who once had to be forced at gunpoint to wait for a shore party which had dallied past his ETD. Astor's proxies on the voyage were two Scots, McDougal and McKay, who were presumed to be company men but were in fact Loyalists. Before they left New York they luncheoned with the British Consulate and apprised him of Astor's plans. The expeditionary team was made up of Canadian voyageurs who, when asked to swear allegiance to the American flag, claimed they already had, which was a yarn.

The vessel sailed from New York in 1811, rounded the tip of South America and hove north to the Sandwich Islands. On the way the Scots took great delight in whispering Gaelic to each other, which Captain Thorn couldn't understand and interpreted as sedition. By the time they reached the mouth of the Columbia, Thorn had retreated into a paranoid fog. Against all counsel he sent a launch into the foaming breakers. It vanished without a trace. He sent out a second boat, and it too was lost. Finally the weather backed off and they sailed up the great river to a headland clearing, where they built Fort Astoria.

One of the locals had picked up a smattering of English from the sea otter trade. McDougal convinced him to come north to Vancouver Island as an interpreter. They set sail on June 5. Once the gunboat was gone, the Natives around Astoria massed for an attack. McKay nervously awaited the *Tonquin*'s return, but in August a group of itinerant Chinook told him the ship had exploded up in Nootka. He didn't believe it until the Native interpreter arrived and filled in the details.

The ship had reached the village of Nahwitty in Nootka Sound without incident. But on the very first day of trading, Thorn got in a fight with Chief Nuk-mis and rubbed a sea otter pelt in his face. Next morning, canoes full of Clayoquots showed up carrying otter pelts for trade. Not only did the crew welcome them aboard, but the idiots began trading them knives. McDougal grew nervous and begged Thorn to weigh anchor, but the captain just pointed at his row of cannons. More and more warriors climbed up the sides of the *Tonquin* until finally Thorn relented and sent five men up the mast to unfurl the sails. But it was too late. The Clayoquots had bought enough knives to turn on the crew. The ship's clerk, Lewis, was the first man to fall, stabbed in the back and thrown down an open hatch. The rest were summarily slaughtered or tossed into the water, where the Clayoquot women finished them off with sharpened yew wood paddles. Within minutes only the handful of men sent up the mast survived.

At their first opportunity these five lowered themselves on ropes right into the open steerage hatch, broke through a bulkhead to the armoury and rushed out onto the deck in a cloud of smoke and pistol fire. The Clayoquots fled. In the wheelhouse the survivors found Lewis, mortally wounded. He suggested that they slip the cable and sail south, but the others decided the westerly wind from Edith Simon's version was so strong that it would drive them onto the shore. When night fell they set out for Astoria in the ship's launch.

Lewis knew he would not survive such a journey, and he didn't want to die by torture. He waited in the wheelhouse until dawn, then lured the Clayoquots back aboard by waving trading blankets. Soon the deck was crowded with braves bent on plunder. Once the party was underway Lewis retired to the powder room and detonated the magazine. The explosion hurled bodies as far as Tin Wis. When the smoke cleared, a hundred braves were dead.

Meanwhile, the crewmen in the launch had failed to clear a point of land against the westerly, so they rowed into a sheltered cove and fell asleep while waiting for the wind to drop. They were roused from their nap by a Clayoquot search party and escorted back to Echachist and a lingering death. The interpreter alone survived because he was connected to the Clayoquots by marriage. He remained among them as a captive for a year, then escaped and made his way south.

This intelligence dashed the hopes of those now stranded at Astoria. It is rumoured that McKay was only able to survive the winter by showing the local chiefs a little bottle that he said contained the smallpox scourge. If he opened it, they would all die. The chiefs at once became his best friends. By this ruse the interpreter's tale of what befell the *Tonquin* was brought back to civilization and written up by both Gabrielle Fencher and Alexander Ross, then bowdlerized by Washington Irving in his famously misleading book *Astoria*. It is the only eyewitness account of the *Tonquin*'s fate, upon which all other histories are based.

Because the interpreter said all this happened at Nootka, divers had been looking for the wreck up there ever since.

But Rod put his faith in Edith's oral history. An explosion like that, only seventy years before she was born, would surely not be forgotten. It would be like us forgetting World War II. Rod moved to Clayoquot, raised a family out on Strawberry Island, named the kids after stuff he saw under the water — Gill, Coral, Finn — and searched the sea floor for thirty years.

One spring day Darin Bostrom snagged the line of a crab trap on something under Templar Channel. Gilley went down and found the line fouled around an iron bar as thick as his arm and half-eaten by salt. From the angle and the texture and a thousand hours spent on the ocean floor, he knew it wasn't just a piece of junk. When he came up he said, "Dad, I think it's the *Tonquin*."

When Rod went down to look, his gut told him Gilley was right. He had searched here before and found nothing, but the sea floor shifts constantly and reveals new secrets. He had dived a hundred times in front of Tofino harbour, and then one day the edge of a bank wore away and he found the wreck of the *Hera,* the aged ship that left Seattle with only coffee and salt horse in the galley. The rusted bar under Templar was exactly the right size and shape to be the tine of the *Tonquin*'s anchor. He reached out and laid his hand on the rotted iron. This was his Holy Grail.

He called the BC Marine Archeological Society and told them he had found an anchor right where Edith Simon said the *Tonquin* went down. There was no reply. Months passed, and still no word. Finally Whitey's son Steve got the Tofino Business Association to cough up some cash, they brought a barge round to Templar Channel, blasted the sandy bottom with powder until the anchor was freed, and hauled it to the surface.

It turned out to be precisely the sort of anchor that the

Tonquin would have carried. Rod took it back to his dock at Strawberry Island. While he was cleaning it up, his two youngest daughters found blue trader beads embedded in the mouldering iron, of the exact type and vintage that the *Tonquin* took on at the Sandwich Islands for trading with the Nuu-chah-nulth. But none of this was proof positive. Many ships lost anchors along this coast during the sea otter trade. Those blue beads are also common. What Rod needed was a cannon, because few vessels at that time were armed to the teeth like the *Tonquin*. But the weather was now too rough to dive.

To keep the anchor from corroding in the air, it had to be desalinated in a special tank. Rod got Fredy Guttman, the local blacksmith, to weld a T-shaped tank at his shop. They immersed the mystery anchor in a special solution and waited for the weather to improve.

Fredy was a Hephæstus character who hailed from Frankfurt, where he worked for a petrochemical giant run by suits he called "the bad guys", welding patches onto huge vats of acid so caustic they corroded constantly. He loved cowboy movies, especially if they were set in the desert, so he took a holiday jumping freight trains across the southern States. One morning he swung out the side of a boxcar just as the train crossed the Rio Grande, and when the desert floor dropped away beneath him and he shot into the blue desert sky he realized Frankfurt was history. He came to Clayoquot for a welding gig and it happened again. The place was no desert, but when he saw the towering walls of trees his heart exploded out of his chest into the scenery. He got a room at Hans Huebner's hotel and never left.

Hans was also from Germany, but from the war generation. He couldn't join the Legion like the other men, so he ended up a bit of a loner. One winter a tree on his property came down during a storm and took out the hydro lines, and he had to pay for the damage. The next year he cut down every tree on his property, which was half of Tofino. His motel coffee shop was so unpopular that I would go there when I wanted peace and quiet.

One morning I ordered toast and coffee. The place was still as a grave and the waitress had gone home, so he brought the toast over himself. "See that land?" He swept his trigger-fingerless hand across the clearcut. "All that land is mine. And this restaurant. And the kitchen. Everything you can see is mine."

"Not this toast," I said. He was furious because he knew it was true. He had sold me the toast, and now — ach! How it galled him! I tried to buy more toast, but he threw the bill on the table and ignored me.

Fredy stayed at the Huebners' for six months, then bought a chunk of land across the highway from the motel and built a house and a metal shop. He had an affinity for metal. One night I watched him repair my old Schwinn bike. The shop was lit by only the wood stove and his torch. He heated the metal till it bent like pasta and banged it into shape. It was a revelation to me. I had thought of metal as gray and unyielding, as final in its form as a noun. But to Fredy, metal was a soft, bright verb and its shape was still open to negotiation.

When I moved forward with my plan to transform the *Loch Ryan* by extending the wheelhouse back over the fish hold, I got Fredy to weld a giant steel collar from two-inch angle plate. I laid the collar on the deck, drew a line round it, took a deep breath, and chainsawed through the beautiful steam-bent deck timbers. I was bolting the collar into the severed beams when Art came by.

"Andrew, you're ruining that good old boat!"

"Well, I'm not spending another winter in that little wheelhouse." I showed him my plan and Fredy's metal collar.

"Oh. That should work."

I hoped he was right. I knew something of the skill and wisdom that had gone into building the boat. I felt like I was trying to improve a Mozart sonata by adding a kazoo finale.

With help from the Sadlers and John Bradford I got the cabin framed in and roofed before the weather broke. The new cabin stretched almost the full length of the boat, with headroom where the deck once was. Pasheabel immediately moved into the new cabin. I asked her why, when the fo'c's'le cabin was so pretty. She said she needed the space.

The final step was fibreglass. Til then I had used the stuff only to fix dings in my surf board and, years earlier in the north of Scotland, to build some kayaks with my dad. The mould we used was taken from an Inuit kayak. We could see marks left by the original wood. The reek of the resin made me sick and the solvent left my hands pink as skinned rabbits. After the dirty work we poured the effluent down a drain that led thirty feet into the North Sea, where the *Aberdeen Rover* fished. That sea is full of oil rigs now, and the economy is going off like a string of firecrackers.

When I glassed my new cabin I used a respirator and a complete body suit, but I still felt sick by the end of the day. At least the cabin was waterproof. She could take a green wave up the side and shrug it off.

I showed Peter. He said, "Art's retiring."

"No way," I said. "He's been here longer than most of the pilings." But two weeks later I came down Main Street with a bag of groceries and saw Art standing on the hill above the docks, gazing down on them with a distant expression, like a man watching his daughter leave for college.

The new wharfinger was Bruce Grant, skipper of the *Wanderer II*. Like most folks in Tofino, he had a live-and-let-live-aboard mentality. "Don't worry, Andrew," he said. "I'm not gonna just move in and make a bunch of changes." But change came anyway.

One morning it blew cold from the northwest. The tide was ebbing fast. A big chunk of blackened flotsam swept past the end of the dock. Then charred timbers and whole walls with electrical wiring and nails started showing up. Lance stood on his boat with a pike pole, trying to keep them from smashing into his hull. I said, "What the hell?"

"Fish plant's on fire!" he yelled.

Lance worked in the yarn department. If you said you'd spent a month slumming in Kathmandu, he said he'd lived there for a year, on the street, as an orphan, with a hearing aid. But today he spake troth. Up the inlet clouds of smoke billowed into the clear blue sky. I ran the *Loch Ryan* over to the fish plant dock. The women from the cutting table were sitting on deck chairs out front, drinking beer and watching the volunteer fire department battle the flames in the ice house. Three young guys stood on the second floor with a hose. Suddenly a wall collapsed, a cloud of smoke and sparks flew up, and the men were gone. The women screamed.

It's a miracle more small-town firemen don't get killed. I was on the Tough City brigade for two years. Sometimes our Tuesday night practice felt like the heart of civil defence, and sometimes it felt like an excuse to escape from our wives and drink the free beer that the restaurants in town provided by the flat. One night we practised on a derelict house near Mackenzie Beach, and afterward we sat at the clubhouse drinking beer, as was our wont. Suddenly all our pagers went off at once. The house had reignited.

The new cop was sitting in his car at the end of the road like a hunter with a pit lamp, and we were all half-cut, except for Crystal's brother Tony, who had only driven the truck once. A crowd gathered to watch the fun as we loaded up the gear. Barry Campbell and Brian Fuller marched across the black-top to the ladder, hauled it up onto their shoulders, turned in opposite directions and tried to march away. Down they went. I clipped my harness to the rail at the back of the truck and clambered onto the footplate. Tony lurched forward and three of us fell off and rattled behind the truck like JUST MARRIED cans. I felt like such a goat.

But then Kathy Lapeyrouse's roof caught fire, and I was first inside with my breathing apparatus on. I stood in her living room, where I had often meditated and drank herbal teas, only this time I had big muddy boots and a high-powered hose. Fire Chief Jim McBride said, "If you see flame, don't hesitate." It got so smoky everyone had to clear out, and I stood alone, watching the hot spot. A flame licked from a crack at the top of the chimney wall. I hesitated, then I gave it hell. Those hoses are powerful. The jet of water thundered into the shelves above the stove, and paperbacks and records flew from the bookcase as if it was one of those automatic letter-sorting machines. We caused a lot of damage, but we saved the house, and for weeks afterward Kathy brought us homemade cookies. I felt like a hero.

Next summer I ran an art gallery out of the top floor of the Schooner. Paul Winstanley had created an installation piece that made paintings out of sunlight. The sunlight was reflected into the gallery from a parabolic mirror mounted outside the back window. When winter came I lost my shirt and closed the gallery, but I forgot to take the parabolic mirror down. Those mirrors are powerful. When the sun came out in the spring, the mirror focused its light onto the cedar siding and set the whole back wall of the Schooner on fire. As we rushed towards the building with our hoses and hats I felt confused. Was I a hero or a goat?

The day the fish plant burned, no one got hurt. When the smoke cleared we saw those three young guys standing on a pony wall next to the ice house. They had jumped back just in time. When they cleaned up the mess, half the fish plant was gone. I had spent nine winters inside, and didn't miss the place, but it was strange to think that our coffee room on the third floor, with its million-dollar view of Meares, and the sauna where we steamed after many grueling twelve-hour shifts, had been consigned to ash. The remains of the fish plant ended up in pieces on the Fourth Street dock, salvaged for extensions on boats that were sinking in their moorings. There were live-aboards on every finger, fish boats with tents on their backs, clotheslines on power poles, drums, carving chips, and giant dogs running up and down the floats. Mark Baston's boat was lashed to the boom log next to Lance, with an orange Co-op extension cord hanging under the water to the power box beside the *Loch Ryan*. The crab dock was worse. It looked like a decommissioned shanty town. You couldn't even get to the far end.

The pressure to ban live-aboards mounted. Down on the first finger the Chinese crabbers still lived on their beer-can boats, but those people were discreet. They didn't drum all night right outside the wheelhouse of a cod fisherman who had to get up at four to catch the morning bite.

"There's going to be trouble," said Peter. He was right. By this time, old-school fishing had collapsed. Every year the Feds spent more money running the show than the industry brought in. To balance the books, the Feds bailed on the wharfinger business. Fisheries started a program to turn the reins over to groups of local fishermen called Harbour Authorities, but because it was a government program, everything had to be politically correct, so these men who fished for a living were now to be called *fishers*. Since 1994 over 300 of the 1,300 federally run harbours had been weaned in this way.

It sounded great. I'm with Johnson, who said, "He governs best who governs least." The Feds organized an orientation session in the room over the pub with free coffee and thousands of dollars' worth of aerial photos of the docks, overlaid with cryptic sentences in huge block letters. All the *fishers* in town stood around in gumboots, drinking coffee and trying to pick out their boats in the photos. There were presentations and discussions, and by the end of the night I still had no idea what a Harbour Authority actually was. Before I could find out, a group of *fishers* elected themselves as Tofino's Harbour Authority, and their first act was to kick all the live-aboards off the docks. I was steamed. I figured the Authority was a bunch of old men who believed if they kicked the hippies off the docks it would be like old times, the fleet would be restored and the salmon would come back. It was as if they were in league with the Feds, part of a plan to squeeze the juice from free radicals like myself. So be it. This was my final battle to stay off the Grid.

But those faceless Authority figures turned out to be the remnants of the Clayoquot pirates: Neil Botting, Rollie Arnet, Whitey Bernard, Art Clarke.

I said, "Art, you're destroying these good old boats."

Art said, "Thing about wood, it rots."

"So you'd rather have fibreglass?"

"Oh yes. Fibreglass boats are better."

Art was a practical man. He loved old wooden boats the way a farmer loves the pig he plans to slaughter in the fall. Jamie Sloman said not to worry, it wasn't the end of the wooden boat world. His boat, the *Loricia,* was in fine fettle. So long as he kept up the maintenance, she would outlast him. And the Sadlers still fished their wooden boats and planned on doing so right up until the end of the world, although according to them that was not far off.

I tracked down Brian Danes, the Fed in charge of harbour transformation. I told him about all the work I'd put into my boat. I said it seemed crazy that you get a huge insurance break if your car from Detroit is an antique, but no support for a fish boat that was built right here with timbers from our own shores. He agreed. I had expected a bureaucrat from Ottawa who had never been fifty metres from a water cooler, but Brian had grown up on fish boats running up and down the coast, and he had loved every minute of it. He had no wish to see the lifestyle vanish. But the federal mandate was to turn these docks over to local user groups, and he couldn't recognize live-aboards as a user group because they weren't supposed to be there in the first place. So the battle to stay off the Grid was going badly, and right in the middle of it my ex-wife Gwen dropped The Bomb.

For years Gwen had lived in a house on Barry Grumbach's land, across a narrow channel from the docks. At low tide Pasheabel could walk there from the *Loch Ryan.* It was a strange old building, up on stilts like Baba Yaga's place. In winter storms the sea washed right up under the floor and sucked flotsam out of the crawlspace. In the garden grew fruit trees planted by a Japanese family who had lived there before the War. Some forgotten redneck artist had painted a Playboy centerfold on the plywood in the back hall. To pay the bills Gwen ran a whale-watching operation out of Rollie Arnet's boat shed, but now tales of a new gold rush had come north from Seattle and Vancouver. Fortunes waited to be made on the Internet. Gwen gave notice for the spring and enrolled at a computer school down in Victoria, which meant she was moving to the city. Which meant *I* was moving to the city.

People were surprised I didn't put up more of a fight. But one thing I don't screw around with is my connection with my daughter. A hidden strength of oral histories, like Edith Simon's tale of the *Tonquin*, is that they bond generations together as they pass from elders to children over ten thousand campfires. A hidden weakness of writing everything down is that it saps strength from that bond, which can have tragic consequences, because children connect a man with the big picture. When the doctor first put Pasheabel in my arms I expected her to be fresh as the heart of a Romaine lettuce, yet here was this tiny, ancient creature, like something from an Egyptian tomb, and suddenly I felt green behind the ears. Five summers later as we walked along Chestermans Beach she said, "Dad — remember when you were the kid and I was the mom?"

Now she lay sleeping on a ragged foamy in the bilge of my boat, like a heroine from one of her beloved books. Soon she would be twelve, and the smell of diesel would become a curse. I knew I had to find a better way of going about things even if it meant venturing deeper onto the Grid.

EIGHT

"THERE'S A GIANT MONOLITH UP ON FLORES!"
said Laser Dave, who once heralded the non-existent
tsunami of '86. These days he ran the dock where the float
planes landed, so he was first to hear the pilots' tales. "It's a
hundred feet tall and there's hieroglyphs down the front."

I was skeptical. But this was the Clayoquot. The line
between the time of legend and the time of day is seriously
blurred. The winter before there had been a spate of Big-
foot sightings at Long Beach. Old fishermen still recall setting hooks for the giant Clayoquot sturgeon, even though
these creatures don't officially exist. If there was a giant
monolith anywhere, Flores would be the place. And though
Laser marched to a different drummer, the beat was pretty
good. One night we walked home from the bar past the last
treed lot on Main Street. The air was foggy but the ground
was dry. When we passed the trees Laser said, "Listen."

There was a gentle prickling sound. It was the fog,
wicked from the night air by the trees and falling to earth as
the gentlest of rains. Laser said, "*That's* a rainforest."

I was thunderstruck. It was like a graduate degree in ecol-
ogy squeezed into a drunken moment. The whole peninsula
was dry except for the patch under those branches. The little
forest was like a last chunk of lung. A year later we sat out-

side the coffee shop and watched those trees come down.

Not long after Laser told me about the Monolith, I was playing tunes with the Bottomfeeders at John Armstrong's house. We picked our way through "Long Black Veil", then Doctor John tossed a snapshot down among the empties and ashtrays. It showed a column of rock that towered above the trees, high on a mountain ridge. He'd snapped the shot on his weekly flight up the coast of Flores to the clinic at Hot Springs Cove. But when he asked around, the Nuu-chah-nulth elders couldn't recall any stories about any Monolith.

It made no sense. Those guys have been here for ten thousand years. They have an epic poem about every boulder. There's a sacred pool in the mountains above Hot Springs Cove where ancient whalers retreated to pray before the hunt. After months of celibacy and weeks of fasting and self-abrasion with sticks and stones, the whaler would climb up to the pool and search for a mussel with its insides showing. If he found one, he would dry the insides and bind them under the tip of his harpoon. This guaranteed success on the hunt. The pool was only a few yards across, and just as remote as the Monolith, but the elders had sung about it for millennia. How could they miss a hundred-foot spire?

But perhaps the Monolith itself was a whaling shrine, and the aura of mystery lay around the place because stories about it had been passed down from chief to son in secret, to preserve their power. Whaling was the linchpin of Nuu-chah-nulth culture, and throwing the harpoon was serious business, because back then whales were people too. They had their own longhouses under the ocean and they put on their great bodies to come to the shore and hunt for food, standing up on their tails at Raphael Point to scrape razor clams from the sand. When the westerly wind blew steady, giant dugout canoes were launched from the flat rock near Hesquiat and forged through the surf, each carrying eight men. The chief stood balancing a yew wood harpoon in the nook of the prow. For eight months he had been celibate. For two weeks he had fasted and prayed in a secret shrine high in the mountains. Back home at the longhouse, his wife lay in a ceremonial bed and prayed for a whale's soul to enter her body. When she caught a good one she kept absolutely still. If she so much as flinched the whale would flinch also, and smash her husband's canoe, or drag the whalers out into the deep ocean.

When the chief fired his harpoon into the whale's flank the mussel shell tip detached, leaving a medicine bag lodged under the whale's thick skin. A cedar bark rope connected the tip to floats made from inflated seal skins, which prevented the whale from diving while the contents of the medicine bag did their work. To stop the whale from filling with water and sinking, one of the men would jump into the water and, breathing through a bull kelp tube, sew up its mouth with a bone tool called a *kacheik*, sometimes translated as "needle", but literally "to push through". Nuu-chah-Nulth don't have a lot of nouns. They're all about verbs, which bodes ill for treaty negotiations. We want a treaty, they want negotiations.

By now I was hooked on whaling, old school. But winter had arrived, and I had other worries. In the spring I would have to take the *Loch Ryan* down to Victoria and figure out how to make a living in the city, and the Grid had me so spooked I didn't know where to start.

One day I saw a note on the wall of the organic store:

TV FOR SALE
SONY — 12 VOLT/110.

It had been ten years since I'd had that kind of entertainment. I loved silence. I was happy that Pasheabel had grown up able to hear herself think, although later she told me there were times when the silence grew so loud she thought she was going mad. But the Sony was a six-inch. The screen was so tiny it seemed more like an inoculation against the hundred channels that would beset me in the city.

I anchored out in God's Pocket for the night and hooked the TV up to the backup battery, which charged off the engine. The only channel was CBC North. I watched the weather from Hay River, then two old trappers talking Dogrib in a faux log cabin, then a couple of public service announcements for dubiously named federal programs like "Women Can't Be Beat", then a man in a parka talking into a wind-buffeted microphone on a snowy waste under a cloudless sky. Either the Feds thought this sort of fare would shore up the Clayoquot's sense of cultural identity, or the CBC had a toggle switch on its desk that said CITY/BOON-DOCKS.

The next morning was Sunday. The rain fell sideways. It was a perfect day to watch TV, but the only thing on was *Coronation Street*. I remembered The Street from childhood. It had started its record-breaking run the year I was born. The show wallowed in all that I feared about the Grid: grey slate roofs, paved gardens, hard lives interlocked like cobblestones. I had spent my earliest years in Africa, and when I got back to Glasgow the place seemed like a wasteland populated by pale ghosts with bad teeth. In Africa, teeth could last for a million years lying in the dirt — but put them in a

Briton's head and they were gone in thirty. It made no sense.

The sad, flatulent horns during the opening credits filled me with existential dread. The episode revolved around a loser named Les Battersby. Half an hour in I wanted to see Les get his comeuppance so bad it was like a drug. Two hours of stupid, ugly plebs tearing strips off each other, and I loved every minute. After the show I watched a sports special about badminton, and before I knew it I was struggling to get back to my bookshelf. I failed. Fortunately the backup battery drained halfway through *Cottage Country*. I had to turn off the TV to keep the bilge pump functioning.

That winter my reading entered a bit of a backwater. I was tired of Joseph Campbell. His Hero's Journey shtick was cool, but what I really needed was something on the Goat's Path. No such tome existed.

The great thing about home schooling is that your learning finds its own course, like a river. Jung flowed into Campbell, and now Campbell talked about some guy called Spengler, whom he called his "major prophet". Turned out Oswald Spengler was an obscure German schoolteacher who quit his day job to complete his thousand-page opus, *Decline of the West,* in a dingy, candle-lit Munich apartment. The book was the hottest title of 1918 but had long since fallen out of vogue because Spengler's philosophy proceeded not by logic, but by a series of intuitive leaps. Linda at the library had to order me a copy from a university in the States.

Spengler saw cultures as organic structures, like trees. The seed of each culture was a metaphor so powerful that it could bind together millions of people for a thousand years. It was their secret name for God. The sapling culture's metaphor unfolded in science and art. At its high point the metaphor hardened from verb into noun, and once every variation of the main theme was played out, the culture withered and fell into decline, hence the gloomy title.

He described the metaphor at the heart of European culture as "a soaring into the wide horizon . . . infinite solitude, steeped in music and the night." He chose the stained glass window as the art form that was uniquely European, because it strove to contain the infinite by capturing light in a flat plane.

When there are ten thousands details in your life, the important connections get lost in background chatter. But there were only two things in my life right then: Spengler and my twelve-volt TV. One night a flash lit up my brain, and I saw the tiny television screen in the nose of the fo'c's'le as a stained glass window that opened on the infinite. No wonder it held us in such thrall. That screen held our culture's secret name for God. Film was the same. A single frame held up to the projector's beam is in essence a tiny stained glass window. This cast new light on something mysterious that happened to me when I was ten.

We had gone up to Edinburgh for the Festival. Mum and Dad wanted to see *Lost Horizon,* a musical about Shangri-La starring Albert Finney. My brother and I bullied our little sister into seeing *2001: A Space Odyssey,* which I thought would be like *Planet of the Apes* because it had the three key ingredients: monkeys, spaceships and the future.

From the opening chords of Strauss I knew there was something different about this movie. Half an hour later I put my finger on it. *2001: A Space Odyssey* was the first boring science fiction film ever made. I had no idea what was going on. It was worse than church. When HAL, the evil computer, went postal and killed everyone, it came as a great relief. At least it would be over soon. Then Dave, the astronaut, got into a pod and went soaring into the wide horizon — infinite solitude, steeped in music and the night . . .

I forget what happened next. When the lights came up I had no idea who I was. I recalled something about a tiny, freckled meat-prison who lived on a speck of dirt at the edge of all this infinite glory. It was me. I staggered into the street, terrified. The city reeked of soot and frying fat. Textures oppressed me. Faces looked like masks. I had broken my brain. This was really bad.

We met Mum and Dad at a restaurant called The Unique. *Lost Horizon* had been a dud. Albert Finney hadn't even tried to sing, he just gazed wistfully at the top of the screen while they dubbed in a tenor crooning his thoughts. Dad asked if *2001* had been any good. My brother said, "They didn't know how to end it." Everyone looked at me. But between the theatre and the restaurant I had become convinced that the world was an experiment run by aliens, whose cruel plan was to mind-fuck me till I snapped and killed a bunch of people to see if they were flesh and blood inside or just robots.

I was not alone. Soon there was a movement to ban the film. Experts testified that the final "star gate" sequence could trigger seizures. One man blamed the movie for the onset of crippling anxiety attacks and started a support group. MGM billed it as "The Ultimate Trip" and raked in a fortune from heads who saw the show night after night, stoned to the bejeezus, and later scribbled cryptic theories about what Kubrick was trying to say. Kubrick told *Playboy* he had been trying not to say anything. "I wanted to create a visual experience, one that bypasses verbalized pigeon-holing and directly penetrates the subconscious with an emotional and philosophic content."

Well, it worked for me. The movie must have sent me into some sort of metaphysical trance state. It amazed me to think this sort of thing was Kubrick's day job. Snuggled up in the wheelhouse that night I thought, If I have to live in the city, that's the job I want.

As a youth I had dreamed of making movies, but I felt stymied because I thought the camera was the heart of the process, and I had grown up mechanically declined. I had tried a couple of times, but every time I got close to an open camera or an unexposed roll of film I broke into a clammy sweat. Now that I had bested the engine of the *Loch Ryan,* a camera seemed like a cakewalk. I felt I had laid my hand on my destiny, like Rod when he touched that anchor under Templar Channel. Making films would be my Holy Grail.

WHEN THE RAINS FINALLY STOPPED I BUMPED into Doctor John at the Common Loafer. He'd flown over the Monolith again, and this time he'd hit his GPS as the plane swooped past. He figured we could reach the thing by taking a float plane to Wilson Cove and hiking straight into the mountains, using his GPS reading like a homing beacon. He had sketched out the route on a survey map.

The Monolith stood on what was once Otsosaht territory. The last chief of the Otsosahts, Luke Swan, was born in 1897 at the ancient capital of Opnit near Hot Springs. Luke whiled away countless boyhood hours trapping humming-birds with slug slime to impress girls and making salmon lures from scallop clams and homemade copper hooks, as boys had done for æons. When he became chief he was the last to hold the whaling harpoon. By then, war and smallpox had whittled the Otsosaht nation down to Luke and his brother Virgil. They were the last two of their kind, hiding out among the giant trees on Flores like a real-life *Gnome-Mobile.* Luke died in 1987, but his grandson Jimmy still lived up in Ahousaht. That would be our next stop.

A few weeks later I found myself in a float plane, hanging

above Clayoquot Sound like a storm god on a coffee break, while below me miles of shattered islands bristled up from a gunmetal sea. The sun came up like the end of a cannon, sharpening every shadow till you could cut your thumb.

Doctor John rode shotgun, his dog-eared survey map on his knees. He was a long way from Ontario, where the trees are so small they stack them on the logging trucks sideways. He too moved to Clayoquot by mistake. He camped at Long Beach on a med school break, and out of curiosity followed a string of H signs to the Tofino Hospital. He never escaped.

Wedged into the seat beside me, Adrian Dorst pulled a lens from a bag full of cameras and craned for an aerial shot. He said he liked to fly with the plane door open. Heights didn't bother him. For years he worked as a steeple-jack back east. Without a safety harness he could do a day's work in two hours. Then he would fritter away the time he had saved, playing cards and drinking coffee in a plywood shed with the rest of the crew. One day he watched a man fall ninety feet to the ground. The foreman ran over to the body and strapped a safety harness on it before the WCB arrived, and Adrian began to think about the road less travelled. When the park at Long Beach opened in 1972 he landed a gig cataloguing birds for the Canadian Wildlife Service. He never left.

Our pilot was Gary Richards, one of Bob Wingen's old crew. Gary didn't talk much, but the pirates told me four different versions of an adventure that befell him after the *Tahsis Princess* failed to make them rich. They fixed up an old plane, either a Beechcraft or a Hercules that had been moth-balled at the airport since the War, and flew a load of oysters down to Seattle. Gary had never flown a Herc and he didn't really know how it worked. Just shy of the airport he turned off the fuel pump by mistake and began losing altitude. He had to bring her down in an alleyway. He sheared off both wings, shattered the windshield with his skull and staggered out of the cockpit dripping blood. The oysters were scattered across the blacktop for miles. Disoriented and behind enemy lines, he jumped in a cab and headed for the border, burned so badly that Neil Botting, his neighbour, didn't even recognize him. But I could tell by the way our plane bansheed over the cathedral treetops on the south end of Flores that the crash hadn't cramped Gary's style.

Ebb tide had turned Matilda Inlet into ten acres of mud spiked with fish boat ribs. The Cessna skipped across the surface like a pebble, past the remains of the *Qiuodgar,* Tom Wingen's failed yew wood experiment. The road up from the dock was gravel and weeds. We picked our way between rusting satellite dishes and salmonberry bushes that peeled back weathered siding. It wasn't a pretty sight, and the Ahousahts didn't seem to care. But if you closed your eyes and just listened, it was beautiful. Quiet as a drowned man's whisper. They didn't even have electricity in Ahousaht until 1972, when the CBC filmed *I Heard The Owl Call My Name* and left their generator behind. In contrast, every room in Tough City had been haunted for decades by the drone of the sixty-hertz bagpiper, and we didn't seem to care.

However, both towns agreed that there was nothing better than a good laugh. One evening as I canoed past Ahousaht, a squall drove me onto the sand spit. The first guy who saw me invited me home, which is par for that course. His house was warm and dry and full of couches. The walls were papered with photos of his nieces and nephews. I thanked him for his kindness. He pointed at a painting of a blue-eyed Jesus on the wall. "That's my master."

An hour later, gentile Jesus had fallen down behind a couch, five guys were duking it out on the deck, and my host was impersonating a water cooler with a Texas mickey of vodka. He jabbed at a string of purple marks on his neck. "My girlfriend did that. She got passionate. Now she's gonna have a baby."

I checked out the love bites. They were intense. "Looks like twins," I said. He laughed and punched me hard on the head. But as the party raged he wouldn't let anyone else punch me, which probably saved my life. Every time the door opened he told the new arrivals my joke. There's nothing the Ahousahts like more than a joke. Back in 1864 the ethnographer Gilbert Sproat noted, "They will give a wrong meaning intentionally to a word, and afterwards, if you use it, they will laugh at you."

Jimmy's porch was quiet. Too quiet. He wasn't answering his phone. Rumour said he was busy hosting an anthropologist from the University of Victoria. After two minutes of knocking he appeared at the door, with a tousle of blonde hair behind one shoulder. It was the anthropologist. Jimmy was surprised to learn we had been serious about trekking to the Monolith. He was still half asleep when we shoehorned him into the Cessna.

By the time we dragged our gear onto the dock at Boomer Cove, the sun was already high. We had to find the Monolith and make it back to the cove by dusk. Float planes don't fly at night because there are no runway lights, and a dark blue kayak makes one hell of a speed bump. But the foliage near the road was impassable. Whenever the canopy relented, wild raspberry and salal bushes had crowded towards the light like paparazzi. It was part of a system. The bushes anchored the soil against the endless rain. Alders took root, and their broad leaves filtered sunlight so that young cedar and hemlock shot straight up in search of sky. This gave rise to tall, straight trees that eventually killed the alders with their shade. But the cycle took a century. To speed things up after clear-cutting, MacBlo had slashed and burned the alders, so a lot of the second-growth timber ended up bent and worthless.

The only way through that prickly mess was a network of bear trails. We felt reasonably safe because it was late summer and the bears had followed ripening berries up the mountains. At least, that's the theory. I was treed by a grizzly once up north, and that critter did nothing according to the book.

After a gruelling, spiky slog the canopy closed overhead and the undergrowth abated. But now we had to deal with the trees themselves. It's impossible to grasp the magnitude of British Columbia's rainforest until you have to traverse miles of it. No one knows how big these trees can get. One Douglas-fir felled in Lynn Valley around 1890 was reported to be over 400 feet tall. In 1886 developers felled a 220-foot Douglas-fir at the corner of Georgia and Granville and built the Vancouver Block, which ended up twenty feet shorter than the Douglas-fir had been. Not until the seventies did the high-rises in downtown Vancouver grow taller than the forest they replaced.

We came down a steep slope to a place where the trees had fallen across each other in a colossal game of pick-up-sticks. My usual method for dealing with such terrain is the bushcrawl: strip naked, drop to the needles and slither. There's always ten inches of crawlspace above the forest floor, and you can reach the most secret of places. Neil McQueen and I once slithered upon an ancient midden near Ahous Bay down on Vargas Island. It was the ancestral home of the Ahousahts before they moved up to Flores. The place was uncanny. You could sense the silent round of years. The longhouses were gone, but there remained a green meadow that rose into strange, steep mounds, like an ocean frozen in mid-swell. Someone told me the mounds were formed by the curves of whale bones buried in the midden soil. That soil is magic stuff, a black loam speckled white with shell fragments, the millennial detritus of village life, whose strata read like the pages of an archeological text. This came as a big surprise to us in Tough City. For years we'd been buying the stuff from a local with a truck, fifty bucks a load, because it made such great flower beds.

But the bushcrawl wouldn't get us to the Monolith. It was much too far to slither. We had to deal with the trees head-on. Two hours into Brobdingnag I paused, tangled in a knot of tree limbs, dangling over a pit filled with dead cedar branches. Those things were sharp. If I fell on them from this height they would have the same effect as a Bengal tiger trap. I avoided impalement by crawling down into the pit. Below the bone-white spikes lay a sandy creek bed, dry from summer and speckled with wolf and deer tracks. A critter causeway. We followed it for a hundred yards until it disappeared under another giant cedar.

Jimmy and I glared up at the mountainous nurse log and scratched our heads. This was ridiculous. We were sweating like fat bayou sheriffs, and we hadn't even started the real climb. No way would we reach the Monolith at this pace. Doctor John sat on top of the nurse log, panting. His pants were shredded and his GPS didn't work at all. It couldn't find the satellites for the trees. "I think I see something," he said.

It was a ravine. At the bottom, a river swept smoothly over black and blue rocks. When we climbed down into it, the vault of the forest seemed to arch twice as high, enclosing the ravine like a longhouse roof.

Captain Cook marvelled at the longhouses he saw when he arrived here, which were framed with timbers so gigantic he could not fathom how they had been raised. Or why. No one needs a tree that big just to hold up a roof. He missed the longhouse's connection to the ribbed vaults of his native cathedrals, although both were attempts to enclose the sacred forest vault. Europe thought in stone. Wood was for farm buildings.

He also misunderstood his hosts' god. They seemed to hold the sacred in low regard, because they were willing to sell their totems for a few coins. Later ethnographers learned the value of a totem lay in the right to display it at various rituals, not in the thing itself. To them, God was a verb, not a noun.

The far side of the chasm was one big overhanging root, but after we fought our way through it the forest opened up. A contour line on Doctor John's tattered map led us onto a saddle between two mountains. We skirted a lake, knee-deep in sphagnum. Through the canopy at the far shore we glimpsed two peaks, but it was difficult to tell which one had the Monolith on top. We chose the slope closest to the north tip of Flores, knowing that if we were wrong there would be no time for a second sally.

Three hours later the trees thinned and the forest floor spread out in a carpet of needles and moss. We knew we must be a thousand feet up when we reached a stand of Douglas-fir, because their seeds have to freeze before they grow. It's called stratification, and it keeps these giants from wandering south of their ecological niche.

Above the stand of fir we found a grove of yellow cedars with curious deep grooves in their trunks. They were culturally modified trees, or CMTs. To an anthropologist they are a culture's fingerprints. For example, a swathe of blackened stumps indicates the presence of *mamaalthi*. The bark of the cedars in the grove had been peeled away in strips, probably by women, who would use the stuff to weave harpoon ropes and hats for their whaler husbands. They climbed up here because the bark had no salt in it and could be pounded soft as butter without losing its strength. If Jimmy's forebears came all this way for hats, they must have known about the great stone column nearby. The depth of the checks left in the trunks indicated the women came here around 150 years ago, at the time of the war between the Ahousahts and the Otsosahts.

Two hundred years ago the Ahousahts lived at that ghostly midden on Vargas Island, where the whale bones slept under grass. Their tribe was so small they used the same word for brother and cousin. Their *ah-hoolthie* — the region where they held *seigneurie* — was all open coast. No salmon rivers. To get rights to a salmon river, they married into the mighty Otsosaht nation, which controlled the coastline of Flores and the surrounding islands. But the newlyweds quarrelled. Relatives were drawn into the dispute. The Otsosahts castrated the Ahousaht chief, sat him on a yew wood stake and dangled his genitals from his nose. The Ahousahts attacked en masse and killed eighty braves. The counterattack was botched when the Otsosahts got lost among the giant trees on the south end of Flores. They retreated to their capital at Opnit, in the cove now known as Baseball Bay.

The wooden palisade at Opnit made it impregnable to open attack, so the Ahousahts made a deal with the Clayoquots, who visited Opnit later that summer. One morning the women rose early. They stood on the roof and banged their pots: "Clayoquot women, get up and make our breakfast!"

It was a sign. Each Clayoquot brave slew the Otsosaht sleeping next to him. By lunch, only two fragments of the mighty nation survived — Jimmy Swan's family, the Manhousahts, who were up in Sydney Inlet at the time; and two of the chief's sons, who escaped to Neah Bay in Washington and became part of the Makah. If the Monolith was a whaling shrine, it made sense that there were no stories about it. Any legends, passed in secret from chief to son, may have perished on that bloody morning in Opnit.

A decade or so after the massacre, Clayoquot became part of Canada. The new lieutenant-governor down in Victoria was Sir Joseph William Trutch. He wrote of the Natives, "I think they are the ugliest and laziest creatures I have ever seen." Because the Nuu-chah-nulth were forever travelling between their summer and winter villages, Trutch classified them as itinerants, which is a fancy word for bum. Since they didn't really use the land, like settlers, he reduced their holdings to one-tenth of what had been set aside to help them retain their way of life. The ancient round was broken, whaling foundered, and the oral tradition that cemented past and present was lost.

A HUNDRED FEET ABOVE THE CEDAR GROVE THE ground broke into mossy chunks. I followed Doctor John along a ridge, gripping the springy limbs of dwarf spruce that might be a century old. Up ahead we heard a cry. Ten minutes later we found Adrian and Jimmy sitting with their backs against the base of a gigantic column of rock.

John pulled out a huge inch tape and started measuring. So analytical. The column was formed from volcanic basalt, which must have cooled slowly, crystallizing into a pillar. The cliffs at the top of Lone Cone on Meares Island looked the same. What made the Monolith unique was that the surrounding basalt cooled rapidly, forming weaker rock that crumbled away into soil and left the column to jut like a stone thumb.

Two blocks of basalt lay tumbled against the Monolith's back like giant dice. Adrian scrambled on top of them to get a group shot and found a narrow ledge that slanted farther up the sheer face. Soon we were all edging along it. Halfway up there was a gap in the ledge. I could see promising hand-holds on the far side, but Adrian turned back. His steeple-jack days were over. So did Doctor John. A shattered shinbone up here would be both irresponsible and inconvenient. Jimmy glanced at the drop, paused, then lunged across the gap and disappeared round the side. I followed.

Around the corner the sun was dazzling. Jimmy hauled himself up out of sight. The top was flat as a table. I sat, feeling the lichens tickle my calves, gazing out across Millar Channel to the Atleo, round to Hot Springs Cove and down the coast to Raphael Point. I could see half my life from up there. At the Sulphur Pass blockade I'm chased naked through the forest by the new cop. In the hot springs I sit, lashed by rain, warm and happy on a freezing February night. Five miles out to sea I shift from foot to foot at the wheel of my fish boat. In a derelict cabin on one of the outer beaches I curl against River, listening to the endless rain.

Jimmy could see his whole history etched deeper in the same landscape. At the mouth of the Atleo, Copper Woman cries so hard that Snot Boy comes out of her nose. At Raphael Point, Jimmy's great-granddad harpoons the last sea otter. Battle cries rise from the palisade at Opnit. In the blue distance beyond Hesquiat, the *mamaalthi* arrive in floating houses. It was an epic moment. And not a cloud in the universe.

I said, "This place is amazing. How come there's no stories about it?"

Jimmy said, "Maybe there are stories. How d'you think we found it so easy?"

NINE

"COME ON DOWN AND ENJOY THE VIEW!" SAID the sign outside the pub. One night, on our way home from play rehearsal, Mike James and I changed ENJOY to DESTROY. We laughed and laughed. Then a light clicked on in the pub office, so we ran and hid in the patch of rainforest behind Barry Grumbach's place.

That forest was magic. The creek that ran into the sea beside Gwen and Pasheabel's house had once fed a dozen giant cedars, most of which had been bucked into chunks the size of tool sheds and tumbled into the gully. The forest canopy had grown back over top, and now the gully was pocketed with caves made out of wood. A cougar made a den in there one year and raised some cubs. Pasheabel loved to explore the grotto with a flashlight.

The creek ran down from Barr Mountain on the other side of Campbell Street. For years I thought only one of the giant cedars still stood, the one that towered above Gwen's house. One morning Barry and I sat on his deck watching eagles flap around the topmost branch, shrieking like evil squeeze toys as they are wont to do when making love. Barry said, "I love that noise. So long as there's eagles in that tree I figure town will be okay." Then he waxed lyrical about his Twelve Step Plan, and how all you had to do was be honest with yourself and the drinking just stopped. I listened to him slur through his polemic and thought, But you're drunk right now, buddy.

Barry had a disease. But it was a socially acceptable disease, so he kept at it until he capsized his crab boat off Chestermans Beach and had to wait for a lull between the waves to get out of the wheelhouse.

That winter Neil McQueen took me into the forest on the other side of Campbell Street and showed me a second survivor from that stand of giant cedars. This one was only ten yards from the pavement, but the forest was so thick that it remained hidden. It was twice the size of the cedar above Gwen's house. A young hemlock had sprung up beside it, and you could climb the branches like rungs. The fork of a giant cedar is called a candelabra. This one was so big there was a little grove of huckleberry bushes and a pile of bones where some critter had set up shop. It was like a floating garden. We sat in the garden, thirty feet above the forest floor, and Neil told me the latest about Nashon.

Every small town has a kid who makes the locals shake their heads. "That boy ain't right." With us it was Nashon. I had known him since he was a kid, just a head of golden curls and a beaming grin. He grew up in a cabin near the highway, behind a boat rental sign shaped like a giant pelican. When he was eighteen he drowned diving for geoducks, and Doug Mousseau had to bring him back with the kiss of life. Nashon tried to get a settlement from WCB, but they did a brain scan that showed there was no damage.

Strange rumours made the rounds. He carved a gun out of wood and kept it in a shoulder holster. He tried to change his name to James Bond. Some jokers on the dock found out they could wind him up like a toy and point him at a place, and he would rob it. He stole the village van, drove down to Victoria, stopped at the Payless gas station, and stole $200 and some candy. Next morning the cops asked the clerk if he saw what Nashon had been driving. He nodded. "It said VILLAGE OF TOFINO on the side. There it goes now!"

Nashon had driven right past the place he had just robbed. When the cops caught him he had eaten the candy and spent the cash on hookers. The cops told the judge, "Don't put him in jail. He's like a sponge." But he got two years, and he came out hard as a boat nail.

Nashon's girlfriend, Shannon, lived across the street from me on Chestermans Beach, and every few days she would ambush me and tell me her life story without stopping to breathe. She had been an Olympic swimmer until she fell out of a second-storey window and hit her head. After that all she wanted was to make a living selling bread-dough art. She knew I'd sold some art, and she wanted to know how it was done. I didn't know what to tell her.

One morning she showed me how she had bleached her hair blonde to match Nashon's. She said she hated it. By noon she had coloured it black, but not with hair dye. I forget what she used, but it looked kind of lumpy. After supper I met her walking down the beach wearing a toque, which she pulled off to show me her freshly shaved scalp.

She bought a new couch for her trailer, but she ordered it from a company that made furniture for hotel lobbies. It was so huge it wouldn't fit through the door. She cut the roof off the trailer with a Skil saw and lowered the couch in by crane. When she and Nashon got together I remember thinking, That makes sense. But they fought all the time. He beat her up, so she got a restraining order. She still invited him over for supper, but now if he didn't toe the line she could call the cops.

Neil and I sat in the tree, looking across the inlet, as he told me the latest installment. Nashon had stolen a launch from the Parks department and set up a freehold on Dream Island, near Fred Tibbs's old place. Then he stole a crate of Pop-Tarts from the Co-op. To cook the Pop-Tarts he stole a toaster from the hardware. To run the toaster he stole a generator from the fuel dock. We laughed and laughed.

One night Nashon bludgeoned Shannon to death, drove out a logging road behind Duncan, cut her up and burned the pieces over a campfire. He threw the pieces into a lake, but they floated, so he buried them under a tree. His lawyer told the judge he had brain damage from the diving accident, but the judge had all the paperwork from WCB that proved he was sane. And he had hidden Shannon's body so well that he was deemed rational. Rational and sane are the same in the eyes of the law. Finally a second brain scan was done. It showed that fifteen percent of Nashon's brain was missing. But by then it was too late.

Every person I talked to about the murder told me a different story. It was worse than the *Tonquin* saga. When the story hit the papers it was pretty black and white. Shannon was an innocent victim, Nashon a repeat offender. But in a small town every life is connected, even mine and a monster like Nashon's. One night years before the murder I picked them up hitchhiking. I drove too fast, and Nashon got all worked up and said I should put mag wheels on my car. It was a Datsun. Shannon toyed with one of his golden curls. "Is he my boyfriend? No. Maybe. I just like to play with him. Like a cat playing with a mouse."

When I heard about the murder, all I could think of was their smiles. How could those two smiling faces end up trapped in this horror show *Babes in the Woods?* Two children with head injuries, lost in the forests of Clayoquot Sound.

Shannon and Nashon. Even their names were twisted out of each other.

Over the next few years the forest around the big cedar thinned until you could see it from the road. Whenever I saw its branches I remembered sitting up there with Neil and laughing about Nashon. Now Nashon was in Kent Maximum Security, and Shannon was under the ground somewhere.

The night Mike James and I changed the letters on the pub sign, we discovered the giant cedar's last secret. You could squeeze through a crack and get right inside. The hollow was so big, five people could stand up in there. Mike's flashlight showed that the chamber rose thirty feet into the dark heart of the tree, and a gnarled root as thick as a man's thigh dangled down the centre like a great umbilicus. It was like being inside Gaia's womb.

One day there was a big wooden sign at the front of the forest that said LEFEVRE AND COMPANY. The land now belonged to Chris Lefevre, the developer who had torn down my old house above the fish plant and built the Fred Tibbs Condo in its place. Mike owned one of the condos, but now he and his twin brother Joe set out to save the tree. They started a non-profit society, set up a website and eventually got on the CBC and in the *Globe and Mail.* The twins were go-getters. They had moved up to Canada from Detroit when they were teenagers. Joe lay on the couch all day watching *Hinterland Who's Who.* He couldn't believe how mellow this new land was. Meanwhile, Mike got a Super-8 from his dad and they started making their own movies.

They still had those movies in a box. The winter I had my revelation about cinema and stained glass, we watched them at Joe's house. They were delightful. Those two made movies like Hillmar Wingen built boats. But I didn't think their plan to save the tree was going to work. I told them my own plan: make a movie, sell it for a million bucks and buy the lot the tree was on. The twins were stoked. We started a production company, bought a Super-8 camera in Vancouver and shot the first roll of film inside the hollow cedar. Joe went to check out the Vancouver Film School and phoned to say that tuition cost $16,000, but at the front desk he'd found a pile of flyers for a ten-weekend course some guy called Rutger ran out of his loft on Commercial Drive.

Rutger was a strange one, even for a filmmaker. His place was a bat-cave, chock full of cameras, lights and flatbed editors. His brain was a compendium of the cinematic arts. He knew every gauge, every film stock, every technological dead end that had been explored.

On the first day of class he sat with a black changing bag on his lap, calm as Whistler's Mother, loading film into a Bolex and answering highly technical questions as he worked. I had begun to sweat just from being that close to a roll of unexposed film and an open camera, but Rutger didn't even have to look at his hands, like me when I gutted a salmon. Once the camera was closed he folded the changing bag away and kept talking, and his hands kept moving, like albatross with nowhere to land, until they swooped down and opened the camera again. I was amazed. I had no idea you could be so cavalier with unexposed film. I was feeling more relaxed with each passing moment. Then Rutger looked down and cried "Damn!" and snapped the camera shut. "I hope that roll isn't fucked."

He spent ten minutes setting up a light on a stand and adjusting the barn doors just right. Then he set up a second light next to it. Then he backed into the first light and threw up his hands and screamed, as if bats were attacking him. He was quite a character, but his style of schooling was just right for me. Ten weekends later I had a template of how to make a movie Wingen-style — writing, producing, directing, editing.

When I hitchhiked back to Tough City, a pickup stopped on the shoulder outside Coombs. The driver said he was going to the government dock in Tofino. I told him that was where I lived, on a boat called the *Loch Ryan*.

"I know that boat!" said the driver. His name was Ron MacLeod, great-nephew of old Joe MacLeod, whose boat the *Muns* lay on the sand at Matlahaw. The MacLeod clan came to Clayoquot from the Isle of Skye in the north of Scotland, fifty miles west of Stonehaven where I played under the hull of the *Aberdeen Rover*. Joe and his brother Murdo were adventurous types, and of army age when the War began. Murdo was in Singapore when the Japanese invaded. He locked his bagpipes in a metal box, buried the box under a banyan tree and fled.

Back in Tough City, Joe had commissioned Hillmar Wingen to build him a fish boat called the *Loch Menard*. She was the first boat to roll down the marine tracks, and Hillmar hadn't ironed out the kinks. She glided majestically down the rails into the waves and rolled onto her side. They took her up to Cannery Bay and loaded her down with rocks, but still Joe's new baby yawed in a figure eight and made him seasick, so he sold her after a year. At least, that's the official story. Rollie Arnet said he never got over the embarrassment of the launch.

When the War reached Clayoquot, Joe joined the Gumboot Navy, a reserve unit of fishermen who patrolled the BC coast. After they disbanded he wanted to get back to fishing, but he had no boat. That winter an old Norseman came down the coast on a troller named the *Norcap*. Joe bought her and re-christened her the *Loch Ryan*. So the name Don McGinnis had been unable to recall was *Norcap*. But no one remembered the old Norseman's name or where he had come from.

THE LOCH RYAN WAS STILL TIED TO THE DOCK in Tough City, but Pasheabel and Gwen had found a little pink house beside the college in Victoria. I couldn't bear the idea of being away from Pasheabel for more than a week, so after I helped them move in I looked through the classified ads:

NISSAN PULSAR
$350
(CD player included)

The previous owner was a heavily tattooed Québecois who lived across from the school. "This car, she burns a bit of oil," he said. "Also, she got no reverse."

"No problem," I said. "I'm never coming back."

He started the engine, and the headlights popped up like chameleon's eyes. A cloud of blue smoke drifted across the playground and followed us around town, and the CD player shorted out whenever we went round a sharp curve, but I figured I could rewire the player and pull it out when the car finally tanked, which might not be long.

"I'll give you three hundred."

"Ya, okay, now just turn the fucker off."

Every week I drove through the pass, picked up Pasheabel and spent a couple of days at my sister Hazel's house near Swan Lake. I found a dock out past Brentwood Bay where live-aboards were technically illegal, but the place was run by an Aussie who shared my disdain for the straight-jacket of government regulations. The marina was in a gorgeous bay lined with old-growth trees. All I had to do was get the *Loch Ryan* through the Graveyard.

When Shorty heard I was shipping out, he gave me the stabilizers from his boat. I had taken down my mast, but I figured out a way to make them work by inverting the triangulation. Shorty was skeptical, but when he came over to examine what I'd done he nodded. "That should work."

I ran the *Loch Ryan* out to the shipping lanes and threw the stabies over the gunnels. She sat on the water like a duck. I felt that I had licked the monster of the mechanically declined for good. It was June, and the waters along the coast were like a millpond. I bought charts for the entire coastline, loaded up with safety gear and supplies, then sat up all night, too nervous to sleep. That was the night this tale began.

But as the hours of darkness slipped away, the breeze that blew through the porthole stiffened into the same kind of June westerly that got the survivors of the *Tonquin* crew tortured to death. At dawn I looked outside. There were whitecaps all across the water to Opitsaht, and Turtle stood on the deck of the *Oldfield,* laughing like a maniac. "Look at this!"

He leaned into the hurricane at forty-five degrees. The gale was so strong it held him up. By noon, the whole west coast was a wind tunnel. I waited for the westerly to drop, but it kept up for three days, so I used the time to check the systems. Everything was running perfectly, but there was a pint of coolant missing from the radiator. I had sprung a leak.

Fishermen love it when the cooling system springs a leak because it gives them an opportunity to experiment. The system isn't pressurized, so you can leave the cap off and add stuff. Bruce Grant said I should crack an egg in there. The egg would get into the leak and cook, clogging it. Shorty recommended pepper. I noticed all these remedies involved stuff from the galley. But Art Clarke figured there might be a crack in the manifold, which had a coolant jacket around it. "Turning to steam and blowing right out the stack."

It sounded reasonable. I dismantled the manifold. It was okay, but the compression gasket between it and the engine was now uncompressed. I needed a new one.

Whitey was retired now, and his son Steve ran the fuel dock, which catered more to sports fishing than to relics like the *Loch Ryan*. I had to get the gasket from Erik Larsen, the pro-logging mayor of Ucluelet, who had gained a measure of fame during the Clayoquot blockades by shouting, "It's time to take the bull by the tail!" I had laughed then, but now I was glad Erik clung to the past. His chandlery had bins and shelves of every fish boat fitting and engine part ever made, including the exact gasket Allison needed. As I prepared to bolt the manifold back to the engine block, I noticed there was a hole in the flex pipe that led to the exhaust.

I had no time to fix it. September had just hit. I drove the Amazing $300 Car down to Victoria and dropped Pasheabel off at her new school. In the classroom doorway she stared at all the kids and bustle and squeezed my hand. I loitered in the hallway. She looked so little at her big desk. Back in the car, I cried. Our long semester of hanging out and yakking about Latin and Shakespeare was over. But when I picked her up at three o'clock, the desks were mysteriously smaller, and it was she who seemed big.

Back at the dock I took apart the housing where the stack came through the wheelhouse roof and pulled the muffler out from above, like a big rotten tooth. I pulled and pulled, and it just kept coming out, three feet of muffler, then four feet of rusted pipe encrusted with asbestos tape, chicken wire, stove cement and God knows what else. I laid it on the dock and stared in horror at what I'd done. The muffler weighed a hundred pounds and was made of five-inch steel pipe. I unbolted the plate that held it to the stack, ground off all the rust and stood it upright beside the manifold. I walked along the shore to Whitey's and bought a new chunk of flex pipe, and when I got back to the dock the muffler was gone.

Stolen. I looked around. Most of the live-aboards had been purged, so the dock was quiet. Nothing moved, except Jamie Bray's giant whale-watching boat *Leviathan,* which had just passed with a load of tourists, leaving a wake like an Irish poet. I began to suspect the wake had rocked the dock so violently that my muffler had toppled into the chuck. I got my wetsuit and mask, weighted myself with a couple of lead bars from the ballast, and plunged to the bottom. It wasn't as bad down there as I had feared. A bicycle, a piece of stove pipe, some rusted tools, and my muffler, lying under some fronds. I tied a rope around it and hauled it onto the dock. Shannon Sadler said, "That happened to me once. Just stick it in a streambed overnight and get the salt out."

The closest streambed was over on Meares, where town got its drinking water. That seemed like a bad idea. Instead I stuck the dock hose in one end and left it running all night. By dawn my muffler looked good, but my engine was strewn across the dock in chunks. It looked like one of the exploded diagrams in my owner's manual. Dew was settling on the pieces. I felt a spasm of panic. How had this happened? A week ago I had been moments away from shipping out.

I cut new gaskets from a sheet, bolted everything back together and turned the key. She wouldn't fire. I tried everything. Nothing. I began to sweat. What if my newfound mechanical aptitude was a delusion? Bruce said, "It's a diesel. If there's a problem, it's got to do with fuel or air." I sat on the transom and thought hard. Fuel was getting in. Air was getting in. Fuel was coming out. Therefore . . .

I glanced suspiciously at the rebuilt muffler, which stood like an abstract African sculpture of bronze and burnished rust at the back of the wheelhouse. I didn't want to take it apart again, but I had to. Where the muffler plate bolted to the stack I had put in a new gasket. The gasket fitted perfectly — but I'd forgotten to cut a hole.

Once the air could get out, she started with a roar. I told Bruce and he laughed. "I just thought of where that coolant's coming out," he said. He figured the bearing cuff on the coolant pump had worn out. I started the engine, dangled upside down into the engine room and watched the pump. I could see coolant dripping from the bearing cuff. The problem was solved.

While I waited for another window in the weather, I organized a meeting at the school and told everyone the latest on my movie plan: raise ten grand, make a short film, shop it around in the city. In a year I'd be back with a million bucks and a crew and trailers full of gear, and we'd make a feature.

Town had been burned before. In the seventies there was so much money coming in from the herring fishery that reality got bent. Japanese packers bobbed offshore with the prices they were paying per ton written on their sides in giant numbers. As fishermen motored towards one packer with their catch, the packer beside it would raise its price. If the fish boat changed course, the first ship would outbid the second, and so on. Some skippers figured they made an extra twenty grand just by going back and forth. Hippies volunteered to clean up the bar at the Maquinna Hotel because they invariably found a couple of crumpled hundreds among the ashtrays and empties. Japanese fish buyers skulked around town in business suits, carrying briefcases full of fifties. "Just a gift," they would say. "Please, remember us when you catch some herring."

To harness this cash tsunami, Bob Wingen built an ice house and a fish plant, and they started packing the herring right in town. The government promised to guarantee a loan of $5 million if Bob would build a freezer plant for BC Packers and hire a crew of Nuu-chah-nulth. Don McGinnis built the structure on spec, and every man in town who could swing a hammer worked around the clock to get it done in time for the next herring opening. The women worked triple-overtime shifts on the herring tables. Money was raining from the skies.

At the end of the season the government changed hands, the new crew welched on the deal, and the bank called in the $5 million loan the very next week. Bob was accustomed to doing everything on a handshake, but to the people he was dealing with a handshake meant nothing, and a written contract less than nothing. The BC Packers plant stood derelict from that day to this, the whole town ended up taking a bath, and Bob Wingen left under a cloud. Three generations of honesty, industry and west coast genius had been brought to an end by some corporate pencil pushers in the city.

But Tough City is always up for an adventure, and what could be more adventurous than making a movie? I sold $10,000 worth of shares in less than a month. Everyone wished me well on my journey into the Grid except Ralph Tieleman, who said, "Struthers, if you go down to the city and make something of your life, I'll never speak to you again." And he was better than his word.

When I told Godfrey I was making a movie, he jumped

up and down and said there was going to be a movie about him, too. He had met a Russian princess who had taken him under her wing. She was a true patron. When he ran out of paint halfway through a mural, she sent a float plane to pick him up. The plane flew him to Vancouver, where the princess waited in a stretch limo with a bottle of champagne. She took him to Behnsen's art store, where he dropped five grand on paints and brushes and wound up back at his studio that same night, drunk and heavily supplied.

Godfrey said the Princess knew the film crowd in Vancouver and could set me up with the right crew, but I shied away. A crew has to be chosen by hunch. According to Rutger, the second-in-command on a film shoot was called the Assistant Director. The go-to guy on the Island was Shamess Shute, a steady sort who had grown up on tug boats and packers around Kitimat, and every spring still fished the herring opening with six of his uncles. I figured if he could survive herring season he could run a film shoot. He had a cinematographer friend called Kim Miles, who handled cameras the way Shorty handled knives. Kim said he'd once worked with a grip from Tofino, a madman who had run up a staggering bar tab then put his rental car in the ditch. It turned out to be Conehead, from my gooseneck barnacle days. It's a small world after all.

BY THE TIME I HAD THE SHOOT SET UP IT WAS late October. I didn't want to leave the *Loch Ryan* in Tofino until the spring, but the weather was already atrocious, and I was busy writing cheques like they were Post-Its. When the cheques began to clear I realized I was going to be five grand short. Ten days before the shoot I got a phone call from Sushil Saini, a writer who came to town during the blockades and lived in a cabin on the edge of Ned Flanders Fields. We met at the pub. She said she had just come into an inheritance, and she wanted to buy $5,000 worth of shares in my movie. I couldn't believe my luck. She said, "Don't worry about it. I'm going to be rich. For five thousand down I can make a million dollars in a month."

She pulled out a crumpled photocopy. It was my old nemesis, the Pyramid of Women, re-christened The Muffin Club and now with a $5,000 ante. Awkward moment. How could I demolish the Pyramid while simultaneously touting my crazy film scheme? Maybe I should just stay mum. But I couldn't. I showed her the math. She thought it over and decided to invest in both the movie and the Muffins.

Now I was good to go. The crew asked for the script, but there was none. It seemed like a waste of time to write a script because I could see the whole movie in my head. It took place in a little fishing village on the west coast, where rain had fallen day and night for thirty years and everyone had gone mad. Any resemblance to real towns or persons was entirely coincidental, but the action unfolded in a big old restaurant just like the Schooner. Even though I had robbed the place and almost burned it down, Maré let me use her restaurant to shoot my movie.

We worked for six days and nights straight. On the morning of the seventh day I looked out the Schooner window and saw that the sky had turned gray. My last night in town, and I had worked through it. A different swan song than I had imagined.

I stamped my feet in the frozen parking lot as the grips loaded gear into the van, then squeezed into my seat between light kits and pelican cases and cans of film sealed up like murder weapons with tape that said EXPOSED. The morning was a hundred shades of gray, except for a patch of sunlight high up on the glacier. Town had never looked more beautiful. Fifteen years in the arms of the goddess, and this morning was my last.

DOWN IN VICTORIA I SET UP SHOP IN MY SISTER'S garage. Her husband, Dennis, worked for the city, but he came from nautical stock. His father had deckhanded on the *Princess Maquinna,* and after the War he had helped bring the ocean liner *Princess Marguerite* through the Panama Canal from Scotland.

Y2K hit town a month after I arrived. We watched the big countdown on TV, then I slipped into the basement and threw the breaker, plunging our happy clan into Stygian darkness. Their wails of fear were music to my ears. For that moment Pasheabel thought her dreams had come true, the pavements would crack and we'd have to go back to horses.

But the wee hours of the new millennium were a bleak time for me. Every morning I got up before dawn, cycled to the overpass and watched the waves of steel below hurtle into the city. Nothing for miles but concrete. Everyone was heading to work, but I had no idea how that was done. I had to face a few unpleasant facts: I was almost thirty-nine, I owned nothing and I lived in my sister's garage. Shipwrecked on the shores of middle age.

When the first big winter storm hit, the *Oldfield* was moored at the hurricane buoys. Chris had sold her to a young guy who had never lived on a boat before. Around midnight she started taking water over the transom. The guy tried to set up a pump in the hold, but the sea was too rough. The deck tilted further each hour until she stood on end with her stern down, and just before dawn she broke up and vanished beneath the waves, a big black boat drifting down into big black silence.

A few nights later I had a terrible dream. The *Loch Ryan* was adrift in Templar Channel. Joe James said he'd run me out to her, but first he had to take a shower. It took forever. When I finally got on board, the wheelhouse was clammy and mildewed, just like it was the first time I saw her. But now water swirled around the galley floor. The engine had been replaced with old gardening tools. Barnacles grew on every surface. I woke with a terrible feeling of guilt. I phoned Joe and asked him to check on her. When he got to the boat the battery had shorted and she had taken water up to the engine block. Another twelve hours and she would have foundered. I knew then that there was only one thing I could do to save her.

I left the city at dusk. By ten my headlights were carving slices through the snow in the pass. Winter was upon me. At the top of Hydro Hill the Fiona Apple CD began to cut out. I still hadn't rewired the player. I groped under the dash and squeezed the bird's nest of wires in my fist, trying to wring out the bad connections like water from a sponge. The music cut back in, startlingly loud. When I looked up, the Amazing $300 Car had already left the highway. My high beams lit up the green, green moss that covered a wall of rock dead ahead. The front of the car crumpled into it like a beer can, and Fiona Apple's keening stopped like she'd been shot.

I undid my seatbelt and got out. The right wing was shattered. The left headlight was winking open and shut like a flirting robot. I tried to push the car back onto the road, but the metal had crumpled against the front wheel and it wouldn't turn. After ten minutes Dan Haley from the fish plant drove up in his truck. We pulled a chunk of two-by-four from his box, levered the metal away from the wheel and winched the wreck back onto the road. I tinkered with the engine until I got it running, wedged the headlight open with some twigs and drove down to the coast.

First I went to Ucluelet to deliver the cover painting for Chris Bennett's book. But the *Scotia Queen* was gone. The wharfinger told me Chris had moved to Vancouver and was working for an outfit called Pot TV.

When I reached the Fourth Street dock it was quiet as a ghost town. Everyone was gone. Shorty had sold up and moved to the Interior. Johnny Madokoro had passed away. The only live-aboard left was Peter. His boat was dark and warm inside. He made some tea, and I told him it was time for me to let go of the *Loch Ryan*. I still loved her, but I didn't want to hang on to her until she went down like the *Oldfield*. That's not love. Did he want to step in?

We shook. His grip was so warm and firm I knew I could never take the offer back. She was gone. I was a landlubber once more.

As I walked up the ramp I felt the weight of youth drop from my shoulders like a gunny sack. No longer would I motor past Flores Island of a morning, captain of my little wooden ship, master of my little wooden soul. I drove to the new parking lot above Barry Grumbach's house and gazed across the harbour up the inlet. The moon was so bright I could see the massive landslides that had opened above the logging roads on Lone Cone and Catface. For the first time, Clayoquot Sound looked old. And there was something odd about the forest across the highway. I fell asleep in my broken car, and when I woke up I realized what it was. The big hollow cedar was gone. The magic forest had been cut down and turned into a parking lot.

TEN

"MOST PEOPLE WANT THEIR OWN TOILET," said Shelly, the property manager at 601 Trutch, as she opened the door to Number Five. Personally, I was thrilled that the toilet was indoors. After ten years off the Grid it seemed almost decadent. The rent was only $290 a month because the lack of plumbing had attracted a clientele of rummies and junkies, and regular folks were afraid to move in. But compared to the bar at the Maquinna Hotel, the place was a Buddhist retreat. Such neighbours didn't bother me.

What bothered me was, this was the very same big old house on Trutch Street where I had lived when I got married to Gwen, fifteen years earlier, before the whole Clayoquot adventure began. If I wrote bookends that clunky into a novel it would suck. Real life is not as elegantly structured as a yarn, because God is a bit of a hack. In nature, water flows downhill — end of story. But a good book must return that water to its source.

Although 601 Trutch's strange gravity was slightly creepy I didn't hesitate, because when Shelly opened the door and I looked into Number Five, it happened again: that mental flash, and the rubber moment stretched out forever, like my first sighting of the *Loch Ryan*.

"I'll take it."

I loaded my bedroll and books from my sister's garage into the Amazing $300 Car and drove down to Fairfield. Near the school a cop pulled me over and bellowed through a bullhorn: "STAY INSIDE THE VEHICLE!"

It was a tense situation, but I knew what to do from hanging out with Mike Poole, who owned the hill where I built the pyramid. One day he showed up in a five-ton Hino truck that he got in a trade for some land. We drove it out to the dump to salvage scrap metal. We were rattling down the highway, smoking a blunt the size of Texas while Poole rambled about cannibalism and Easter Island and aliens, when suddenly I realized the new cop was racing along right beside us with all his lights flashing.

I figured we were going straight to jail, but Poole refused to give up hope. The new cop said the Hino's headlights were smashed. Poole said he never drove at night. The new cop said the tires were bald. Poole said replacements were on their way from Port. The new cop said the pullman arm was shot and the Hino might lose steerage at any moment, so Poole had better drive this wreck straight back to town and park it until he got it roadworthy. Poole nodded, then asked if he could drive back to town via the dump. The dump was five miles farther down the highway. Even I couldn't see how it was on the way. But the cop sighed and waved us on, and an hour later we were loading an old TV onto the flatbed.

So I was not afraid when the cop who had pulled me over in Fairfield began to circle the Amazing $300 Car. The right headlight was torn out. The starboard running light dangled an inch from the blacktop. The engine block was clearly visible through the crumpled hood. He couldn't believe I was driving this wreck. I said, "I'm from Tofino." He still couldn't believe it. Then he said he had surfed Long Beach years ago. I said it was really crowded now. He scribbled something on a pink slip of paper and said I had thirty days to get the vehicle roadworthy.

A month later I fished the pink slip out of the glove compartment and wondered if those thirty days included the day I got busted. If so, then today I was over the line. I phoned all the wreckers in the Yellow Pages, but no one wanted the car, not even as scrap. Finally a boneyard out in Sooke said they'd take it off my hands, no charge.

On my way up the Old Island Highway I came round a corner and drove right into the heart of the biggest roadside check in history. There must have been thirty cops buzzing in bumblebee jackets. They were sliding mirrors under chassis, writing up tickets and checking licences. They had pulled over a dozen vehicles or more. But at the moment I ran that copper gauntlet, every single one of them was busy. Not one of them met my eye. It was like a dream where you walk around town naked and nobody notices. It seemed like an omen, but I couldn't figure out whether it was good or bad. Either I had to change my pirate ways or stay the course.

Now I had no boat and no car. Luckily, 601 Trutch was only a couple of blocks from Cook Street Village, which had an organic grocery, a coffee shop and a video store — everything I needed. I walked down to the sea and along the cliffs and met Maquinna, Adrian Dorst's son, coming the other way. He had grown up partly on the reserve at Cape Mudge, and now he had a foot in both worlds. He told me this whole area was once a vast Songhee camas farm. Camas is a kind of tuber, and was a staple of the Native diet. The Songhees traded the stuff up and down the coast, to Clayoquot and beyond. When the *mamaalthi* arrived the open leas reminded them of an English meadow, so they called it Fairfield. Along the banks of the stream that was now Cook Street they planted chestnut trees, and these had since grown into giants, so that Cook Street Village felt like the heart of a forest. The coffee shop, Moka House, took a proactive approach to global warming, heating the porch outside at night so you could sit there with a cup of high-end java and stare up through the glass roof, through towering chestnut branches, at the stars. The video store across the street, Pic-A-Flic, was a treasury of classic films, foreign flicks, cults, docs, and stuff so strange it didn't seem legal. But the strangest part of the Village was the diaspora of Tough City refugees that had collected there.

Raging Betty Krawczyk lived in an old green house with a big front stoop right on Cook Street. We met at the Moka House and compared notes. She had left the Clayoquot shortly after she sold the *Loch Ryan,* but the city hadn't cramped her style. She went blockading at the Elaho Valley, where a mega-corporation was logging a Native burial ground. A judge told Betty to sign a paper saying she'd stay off the logging road. She refused. She asked Premier Dosanjh to call off the goons because she was seventy and a grandmother. He refused, and she spent the next six months in jail. When she got out she ran for the Green Party in Dosanjh's home riding. He begged her to call off the Greens because they were shaving away just enough of the left political sideburn for the Liberal candidate to squeak in. She refused, and that was the end of Dosanjh.

Sushil Saini, whose inheritance had saved my film shoot, lived just across the park in James Bay. She was now the food writer for *Monday* magazine. That Christmas she thought she had found gold in the Pyramid of Women when the Muffin Club threw a top-secret party at an Oak Bay mansion. Fine food, great music and a hundred women from all walks of life, from the welfare rolls to the former attorney general's wife. Initiates testified how the Pyramid had brought wealth into their lives. The ringleaders cursed capitalism as a tool of the patriarchy and swore no man would ever infiltrate their sisterhood. "Men are all in it for themselves, but women support other women."

To raise the five grand, inductees were advised to draw cash advances on their Visas, establish lines of credit and sell their cars. One re-mortgaged her house. Anyone who tried to do the math was told she was a victim of the male myth of scarcity. In the end, all those women took a bath together. Two of the grand poobettes landed in court, shocked to find they had broken the law. But Section 206 of the Criminal Code is pretty clear: such schemes are illegal if you get more money out than you put in due to the participation of others.

Mysteriously, our whole economy is based on bucking Section 206. In theory, the stock exchange takes capital from fallow accounts and ploughs them into the fertile ground of research and development. In fact, many investors buy low and sell high. Their profit comes from the participation of others, who buy high and sell low by mistake. And though the Pyramid of Women requires infinite growth to function, so does the economy. Technically, zero growth is a recession. Perhaps the Pyramid was forbidden because it was built on feminine principle. Doing the math never worked as a deterrent because the inductees were not thinking in those terms. They were thinking about the friend who brought them in, and the other friends they could help. It was as if the connections between the bricks were more important than the bricks themselves. Regardless, the Pyramid had vanished beneath the sands once more. But I knew we'd meet again.

Behind Pic-A-Flic, Godfrey had converted an old wooden garage into a workshop stuffed with paintings and carpeted with cedar chips, half-smoked cigarettes and crumpled tubes of paint. The workbench was hidden under ancient tools with hand-carved handles. A paint-spattered tape deck rasped out Coltrane. It was as if a chunk of Catface had landed in Fairfield. When I dropped by he was carving wooden tears into a giant sculpture of the Nuu-chah-nulth goddess Cedar Woman. He pointed at a gleam in her mouth. "That's Rod Palm's tooth," he said. "We were on Strawberry Island, and he pulled out his tooth with some pliers and I said, Rod! Give me that, and *tap-tap-tap!*"

Behind the studio his daughter Aija lived in a big white building with Tudor fascia. She worked for Fisheries now, going out to sea for a month at a time on the research vessel *Tanu.* One day they saw a Japanese glass float in the water. They turned the ship around, five hundred tons, and fished the float onto the deck. When she told me the story I wondered what else that glass float had seen. It would be wonderful, I thought, to trace its journey back across the vast Pacific, through storms and solitude, all the way to Japan and the little fishing village where it was made.

That sort of mental flash fascinates me. One moment the idea is curled up inside your head. The next a million dollars is being spent on a movie, with trailers full of gear, and fifty people running around.

Down towards the sea on Bushby Street, Crabber Dave had bought a fixer-upper with the money he got from selling his crab licence. He invited me over for a beer, but when I got to Bushby I realized I'd forgotten to ask his house number. In Tofino we called the houses by name. Here, all the houses looked identical: Tudor fascia and manicured lawns. Then I came to a house with waist-high grass against an unpainted fence, and a boat on a rusted trailer. This must be the place.

"Welcome to Fairfield," said Dave as we chinked beers. "It's good here, so long as you can find work."

BUT I DIDN'T NEED WORK. ALL I NEEDED WAS to show the right people my short film. Kevin, the micro-light pilot from the trailer park in Tough City, hooked me up with his school chum Charlotte Mickie, now chief head-hunter at Alliance Atlantis and a genuine Player. She liked my "hook" (*Beachcombers* meets *Twin Peaks*) and she was coming to Vancouver for the Trade Forum, a three-day schmoozefest where the Players and Wannabes of the west coast film world met to talk shop. Also in attendance: indie auteur Don McKellar of *Twitch City.* I thought, Who knows? Maybe me and Don will meet at one of the parties and hit it off. So I scraped up my last few shekels, bought a $300 Forum Pass, grabbed the cover painting for Chris Bennett's book, and headed for the ferry.

Chris was out of town, but Pot TV impresario Marc Emery met me in a diner off Hastings and picked up the painting. Then he launched into a detailed description of how his pot empire worked, firing facts into the air like a drunken bandito. It cost him a million bucks a year to run Pot TV and his magazine, *Cannabis Culture,* but he got lots of free advertising for his pot seed business, which raked in a million-five per annum. The key to his success was that he always paid his taxes. He came off like a pot-smoking Republican, but I liked his freebooting attitude.

The Trade Forum was the opposite of freebooting. There was an entrenched pecking order that would shame a troop of baboons. We were sequestered under the law courts in a cement bunker designed to withstand Ragnarök. The Players' hi-tech cell phones worked inside the bunker, but the Wannabes were all on Fido and had to take their business outside. This demographic became poignantly clear when the rain set in. By lunch you could tell how far down the food chain a person was by how soggy they were.

Joseph Campbell was mentor to all. Ever since George Lucas fessed up that *Star Wars* was based on Campbell's work, the Hero's Journey had become big business — except for the part where old Joe said that the essence of western art was the song of the individual soul. Every panel discussion, every lecture and meeting somehow got around to mentioning that film was a "collaborative art".

The parties were a page from Dante. Everyone was dressed in black, sweeping round and round a mountain of brie, penned in by giant chunks of faux marble, steel, and chiaroscuro plasterwork. The Players had vaselined their eyeballs in case they made eye contact with a Wannabe and found themselves drawn into a pitch session. The appa-ratchki were *giving away* cappuccinos. Bad juju for this boy. I downed three, four, five, muttering, "Dance, little system, dance!" while a tiny man next to me chirped about how he'd just sold a Bruce Lee action figure on eBay for $1,500. Char-lotte Mickie came spilling out of a seminar and recognized me from my press kit. She grabbed my arm and said, "I have to go to the toilet."

Taken aback, I spun round and saw Don McKellar right beside me. I grabbed his arm. "Hey, I loved *Twitch City*."

McKellar gulped like he'd just scarfed a mile-long self-esteem pie and tried to get away. "I have to fly to Calgary," he said. "I only have an hour left."

"Make the most of it," I said. It came out grim, like a warning. Fuck, I thought, that's just the sort of thing a stalker would say.

Next morning I waited for Charlotte in the violently

overblown lobby of the Hotel Georgia. She came racing across the marble floor, pulling a giant suitcase on wheels, moving so fast she didn't show up on the hotel security cameras. "I have to catch an earlier plane," she said. Earlier than *now?* I thought. "Didn't you get my phone message?"

I hadn't. I was on Fido. She squeezed in forty minutes anyway. She was very kind. By the end of it I could see exactly where I'd gone wrong in the making of my film, which was at square one, when I hadn't bothered to write a script. The last thing Charlotte said was: "It's all about the writing." Despite her velocity, she seemed like a steady sort. I thought, If only I knew how to write.

But the only thing I had written was *The Green Shadow,* and that just sort of poured out of me. My only schooling had been a creative writing class in Prince George many years earlier with Al Anderson, a gaggle of alcoholic Amway dropouts, and a guy who got his arm torn off at the plywood plant. The prof was a poet named Barry McKinnon. His first lecture was a rambling discourse on the futility of art in modern culture. After class I told him I felt depressed. He nodded. "D'you like to drink?"

We walked down a back alley to the Yellowhead Pub and ordered a tabletop of beer. Barry said he used to live with the Irish Rovers, until the curly-headed one slept with his girlfriend. Next night he drove to their Burnaby duplex, tugged a huge rock out of the flower bed and hurled it at the front door. The Irish Rovers came spilling out. They were furious. The burly one threw Barry over the hood of his car, then the one with the goatee called the burly one off. "He's got a broken heart," he said, and the others nodded and filed back inside.

I laughed and laughed. Another tabletop of beer arrived, the foamy golden ovals stretching away forever across the red terrycloth. I forget what happened next. I woke up on my parents' living room floor in a pool of my own vomit. At the end of the semester Barry said, "You write pretty good, just keep it up." But he didn't go over any technique. Twenty years later I still had no technique. So I went to the library and took out a whole shelf of how-to books.

I read everything, from Richard Joseph's brassy *BEST-SELLERS!* (Over A Billion Books Have Been Sold By The Writers Inside!) to the tiny, dog-eared *The Neglected Genre: Short Story Writing In Canada,* which almost had me in tears, so unlikely did it seem that I'd ever make a penny from my craft in this godforsaken literary wasteland.

But every book contained a pearl. From Dianne Doubtfire's *The Craft Of Novel Writing* I learned to get up at four and splash cold water on my face. From Stanley Schmidt's *Writing Science Fiction* I gleaned that too much alien jargon bogs down the narrative. In Debra Dixon's *Goal, Motivation and Conflict* I discovered that every character must want something badly (goal) or he'll be in deep shit (motivation), but no matter how he tries, he can't get that thing (conflict). For example, I badly wanted to make some money from writing (goal) because rent was almost due (motivation), but I was still reading these damn how-to books (conflict).

The thickest of the books, *Writer's Market,* was the most important tool in a freelancer's kit. It said so right on the jacket. Inside was a huge list of all the magazines and book publishers in North America, plus insider tips:

1. It's easier to get a publisher once you get an agent.
2. It's harder to get an agent than it is to get a publisher.
3. Write a query that zings.

And so forth. But the library copy of *Writer's Market* was

dated 1996. I didn't want to write a query that zinged to an editor who might have been dead for years, so I went to Munro's Books to check out this year's model. Forty bucks! And I was almost broke.

Shelved beside *The Writer's Market* was a much thinner, much cheaper volume entitled *Online Markets*. The dust jacket claimed *Writer's Market* was obsolete, but with *Online Markets'* know-how I could write on the Internet instantly. I decided to experiment. I e-mailed a query that zinged to Howard Druckman, editor of a music e-zine listed in *Online Markets*. Then I printed out the same query, walked down to the Village, spent two bucks on stamps and mailed it to *Saturday Night Magazine*. When I got home, Druckman had already replied. Wow. He must have been crouched over his Mac like a trapdoor spider. Only it wasn't Druckman — it was some guy called Brophy.

> Hi, Andrew. I killed Druckman and threw his body
into Lake Ontario months ago. Anyway, I'm interested.
But pay is virtually non-existent.

I sent Brophy the piece and he never wrote back. Neither did *Saturday Night*. So far I'd made nothing writing on the Internet and nothing writing in print, although I'd made nothing a lot faster using the Internet. As rent loomed I became despondent. I stopped getting up at four and splashing cold water on my face, unless you count four in the afternoon. I lay in bed till sundown, eating Mr. Noodles, watching reruns of *Blind Date* and receiving from myself what a monk would call "unnatural caresses".

Those how-to books all agreed on one thing: think of the editor as a friend who wants to see you succeed. They were speaking metaphorically, but in my case it was a fact. My best friend in town was Sid Tafler, who had run *The Green Shadow* back when he edited *Monday* magazine. He took me for lunch with the new editor of *Monday,* a young guy called Ross Crockford, who showed up at the sandwich shop in a bicycle helmet and Clark Kent glasses. I asked how long it took to get paid for a piece. He said about six weeks. I was desperate for cash so I put my writing plan on a back burner and buckled down with the classifieds. It was horrifying. Construction, nine bucks an hour. Steam-cleaning carpets for minimum wage. Telephone canvassing on commission. How could people survive in this city?

Only one ad sparked my interest. The Fringe Festival was looking for a manager. I'd never managed a thing in my life, including my life, but at least it was interesting. The voice at the other end listened suspiciously to my pitch and said, "Andrew? Is that you?" It was Ross Crockford. His room-mate was the departing Fringe manager. "They're looking for a bank clerk type," he said. "If you need money, why don't you write a feature for *Monday* and I'll give you an advance."

I cashed the cheque at Western Union, paid my rent and headed down to Future Shop with the balance. I bought the fastest computer they had and hooked it up to the Internet. The Web was amazing. It was like the mysterious membrane that connected Clayoquot, except turned to concrete. It made the writing life so much easier than when I had written *The Green Shadow* just five years earlier. I researched the Mifflin Plan on the Web, wrote a piece about trying to save the *Loch Ryan* and sent it to Ross by e-mail. *Ka-ching!*

I noticed on my Internet news service that *Coronation Street* had now been on the air forty years. I e-mailed the *Vancouver Sun* a pitch for a story about *Coronation Street*'s fortieth anniversary special. The editor was a guy called Jim

Sutherland, he loved the piece, and the *Sun* paid twice as much as *Monday*. Just as that cheque ran out, Sid Tafler called. He had met with a literary agent in Vancouver named Woody MacRoberts. "He keeps a low profile in case he gets flooded with queries. But he wants to meet you. Just come up with an idea for a book."

I fiddled with my *Loch Ryan* feature until it looked like a book outline and headed to Vancouver. Woody held court in an unmarked building off Granville. The outside was discreet as a brown paper bag, but inside a drop-dead secretary sat behind an antique desk flanked by photos of Woody's clients — Pamela Wallin, Rex Murphy and the rest of the status quo. Woody talked *sotto voce* and glanced around nervously, as if he feared that unsolicited manuscripts might suddenly fly at him from all directions. He loved the *Loch Ryan* idea.

Later I had breakfast with Rolf Maurer, who years earlier had published *The Green Shadow*. I told him the good news about Woody and the *Loch Ryan* book. Halfway through his toast, Rolf said, "That sounds interesting. I'll publish that."

"Deal," I said. "But this time, no interviews." Two weeks later he mailed me an advance, a day ahead of rent.

None of this was working out anything like in those how-to books. When I did the math I could see why. There were perhaps 100,000 freelancers in North America. *Writer's Market* sold 4.3 million copies. It said so right on the jacket. That meant for every wordsmith who lived by his pen, some forty tortured souls gleaned a steady harvest of rejection slips. The real winners were the publishers of *Writer's Market,* who raked in millions hawking the dream of the writing life.

It was an easy sell. Writing was a ticket to the Fortunate Land, a promise of limitless opportunities, a bridge across the great divide between rich and poor. In the city you couldn't go fishing for food or build a place in the forest, so the poor suffered terribly. Nowhere was the divide more apparent than between upstairs and downstairs at 601 Trutch. The lower floor was home to a yuppie couple who drove a Miata and carried tennis rackets everywhere, a guy called Chris who was part-owner of Rebar restaurant, big with the wheatgrass crowd, and an older fellow, Drew, who sold etchings and prints. The plumbing-free zone upstairs was a different story. The cops came round so often they were on a first-name basis with the rock 'em sock 'em couple in Number Four. One night I woke to the sound of shattering glass. The mysterious loner in Number Three had thrown Chris from Number Two through the little hundred-year-old window on the landing. I had to intervene with the fish bonker from the *Loch Ryan*.

After that the Miatas in Number One moved out. As I helped them carry their Tupperware to the car I was surprised to find their rent was only $575. Terror must have driven down the price, because the place was grand. Twelve-foot ceilings, elegant plasterwork, two tiled fireplaces, and a bay window that looked down over the manicured gardens. I called Shelly the property manager and snagged it.

Number One held clues to a former glory that belied the flophouse upstairs. Some mornings the last century rose like a fog and revealed the bones of an older city. When the trees out front sloughed off their leaves I could see right down Collinson Street to the flagpole at the Legislature. When I pulled up the hideous carpet in the dining room I found quarter-sawn old-growth fir underneath. I sanded the wood until it glowed like honey. The grain was as tight as the top of my guitar. Who built this place?

I might never have found out had it not been for Pashe-abel's obsession with history. She was halfway through sixth grade and hating every minute. "Why are the kids so cruel to each other?" she asked, and I chuckled because I had no answer. Every day at three I picked her up and asked her where she wanted to go. Usually she chose the library. Thanks to Linda White she felt most at home surrounded by books. After the humble selection in Tofino, the endless stacks of the downtown branch thrilled her. The first time we went up to the university library she almost swooned.

One afternoon around Halloween she wondered if there was a ghost in her mom's house, and if so, what was its name? She looked up her mom's address in the land title registry and discovered the house had been owned for many years by someone named C. Bright. Then after 1953 the title began to change hands rapidly. In the death registry she found an entry for C. Bright, who left this vale of tears in January 1953. In the *Times Colonist* microfiche she found a 1953 obituary for Caroline Bright, who had died in the house. So if a ghost showed up, its name would probably be Caroline. In the car on the way home she told me she had failed her science exam. "I don't have a scientific mind," she said.

The house on Trutch was from the nineteenth century. Pasheabel was certain there must be at least one ghost. At the library we found a book with a drawing of our house. It had been built in 1861. The only house in the whole city that was older was Tod House up in Oak Bay, but it had been rebuilt. It turned out that Collinson ran from the front door down to the Legislature because it was once the house's carriageway, and the man who built the house was the first lieutenant-governor of BC, Sir Joseph William Trutch, the pommy bastard who had gypped Jimmy Swan out of his *ah-hoolthie*. I lived in Hitler's living room. What a spot to drop anchor.

I pored over newspaper clippings and archived letters that painted the place as a west coast Camelot, with cows and horses grazing under the trees, and flower beds and orchards all around. Inevitably, Trutch became human. I found a photo of the house from 1870. Trutch stood on the lawn out front with a croquet mallet and his family. He looked like a steady sort. He had come to the New World in 1849 to build an iron warehouse outside San Francisco. He hated America but found Victoria to his taste. To get cash flowing he built a suspension bridge near Spuzzum and collected $140,000 in tolls at a time when milk cost twopence a gallon. In 1860 he wrote his mother, Charlotte, in England: "I have acquired a most beautiful piece of land, about 10 acres on the skirts of Victoria, and commanding a lovely view."

Charlotte was advanced in years, having heard the news of Napoleon's defeat from Wellington's dispatch rider — from the horse's mouth, as they said. But she was tough. She and her daughter Caroline sailed down to the Mediterranean, crossed the desert by camel to the Red Sea and journeyed via India to the west coast. Charlotte loved sunsets, so the house was built facing west. No expense was spared. The spiral banister in the hall was turned from Spanish mahogany and brought around Cape Horn on a clipper ship. The finished house was named *Fairfield,* Victoria's first grand residence.

Once the home fires were burning, Trutch sailed up to Bella Coola with Governor Seymour to referee the war between the Tsimshians and the Nisga'a. Seymour perished en route, and Trutch returned with the body in a canvas sack and shouldered Seymour's responsibilities. He dreamed of making Vancouver Island a sovereign nation, but as the years passed it seemed annexation to the States was inevitable. Trutch so hated the memory of his San Francisco sojourn that he gave up the dream of independence and in 1867 led a delegation to Ottawa to negotiate entry into the Dominion of Canada.

For Sir John A. Macdonald, Trutch was a godsend — anti-American and an engineer to boot. Just the man to complete his vision of a railroad from sea to sea. Trutch was made BC's first lieutenant-governor and immediately got to work disinheriting the Clayoquots of their land. It's ironic he found them ugly and lazy because if they hadn't blown up that Yankee gunboat *Tonquin,* his beloved Island would already have been whistling Dixie.

He was knighted Sir Joseph in 1890 and lived at Fairfield until 1895, when his wife Julia, who had been diagnosed with indigestion, suddenly died of it. He returned, broken-hearted, to England, where he was thrown from a dogcart into a snow bank, lingered a few years, and died in 1904.

I found the story fascinating, and so did Jim Sutherland, who had left the *Sun* and was now editor of *Western Living Magazine.* They paid in advance. The cheque arrived just before Christmas, so I splurged. Pasheabel decorated the apartment with a yore motif, and by Christmas Day the place looked like an illustration from a Dickens novel. We had a ten-foot fir tree in the front room and a goose for dinner. The angelus rang out across the treetops from Christ Church Cathedral. Presents under the tree, stockings above the fireplace — this wasn't how I had pictured city life at all. I had set sail for the Grid afraid that it would mean the end of mystery, and by some strange mystery ended up in the very room where Trutch had hammered out his plans for the last station of the National Dream.

ELEVEN

"NOTHING STOPS MACDONALD'S FURNITURE!" said the sign in the window of the old MacDonald's furniture store on Pandora Street. Under the banner stood a life-sized cutout of Eddie Albert. He stood there for years, the whole time I was at university. No one seemed to know why. That's the mystery of a big city. Ten million moving parts, and if the connective tissue gets shot, no one knows what the hell's going on.

One day Eddie Albert was gone. CHUM television, a mega-corporation from back east, had bought the building, cleared out the furniture and upgraded the walls to withstand the next tsunami. They called themselves The New VI, but they broadcast warmed-over *Buffy* from the old MacDonald's building, so I called them New MacDonald's.

Not long after they arrived, New MacDonald's sent every filmmaker in town an e-mail. The subject line read: WANNA MAKE A MOVIE? This looked like my big break. All I had to do was send in a script and they'd spend a million dollars turning it into a feature film.

The mass mail-out showed how little these Toronto folks understood the Island. Victoria's film community was so small we were like a family. Moments later the same e-mail was forwarded to me by Michael Giampa, who I had met in a screenwriting class that summer. Then again by Ross Crockford, then by Peter Campbell, my moviemaking mentor.

Peter was a steady sort who had worked his way through film school mining nickel a mile under the Canadian Shield. Now he ran a little production company that made socially relevant docs out of an ancient brick building in Chinatown. One night I told him my idea for a film that followed a glass fishing float back across the Pacific to Japan, and he loved it. Months later we crossed paths outside Pic-A-Flic. He had just met with the National Film Board, that branch of the federal government that handles the cinematic arts, and my glass float idea had popped into his head, so he had set up a meeting for me with a woman at the NFB named Rina Fraticelli.

Rina had just come from back east to head up the office in Vancouver, and she was still awestruck by the beauty of the west coast. The week before we met she drove out to Long Beach and found a glass float washed up on the shore. When I arrived at her office, the float was sitting on her desk. It seemed like a good omen, and it was. She recommended my film to the Board's producers. One of them, Erik Eriksen, had spent his boyhood on the BC coast, where he whiled away countless boyhood hours searching for glass floats on the beach. He picked up my proposal and ran with it, which is a figure of speech movie people use.

I went to Godfrey's carving studio to tell him the good news and thank Aija for the flash of inspiration. Godfrey was massively depressed. He had fallen from grace with the Russian princess. She had taken him on a luxury tour of the Island, shelling out $200 for hotel rooms. Godfrey begged her to give him a hundred of it and he'd sleep in the van. She refused. Everything had to be first-class.

When they got back to Victoria she took two hundred of

his drawings, sculptures and paintings, his entire life's work, to her gallery in Vancouver. Later she showed up with a bottle of champagne and a contract that would make him her art slave for life. He refused to sign and asked for his paintings back. She said first he had to repay all the money she'd put into his career and gave him a $30,000 bill for the plane flights to Vancouver, art supplies, hotel rooms and so forth. He spoke to a lawyer. When she heard that, she bumped the bill up to $200,000. He couldn't pay. "The worst part is, she got all my baby photos," he said.

He was working furiously on a new canvas as he spoke. He was heartbroken about losing his life's work, but he figured he got off light. His friend Jori had worked at the coastguard in Tough City for two years and put every penny into building a yacht so that he could live his dream of sailing around the world. The finished boat was a masterpiece of brass and oiled mahogany. When he set out for Australia his first port of call was a friend's house near Victoria. A Chilean sub with American navy officers on board was performing top-secret manoeuvres in the bay. The periscope cut Jori's boat in half, the pieces went down in less than a minute and he escaped with only his shorts. At least Godfrey still had his art — so long as you consider art to be a verb.

Vancouver Island has a thousand tales of nautical disaster like Jori's. The downtown library was full of them. In the preface to an out-of-print book about shipwrecks I came across a reference to an article about the *Tonquin* that ran in the 1928 *Vancouver Province*. Amazingly, the university library still had that old newspaper on microfiche.

The article turned out to be a second eyewitness account, which was told to Jason Allard, son of the Hudson's Bay factor in Fort Langley during the 1860s. Allard had whiled away countless boyhood hours talking with the Native water carrier at the railroad yard, an old man named Ten-ta-coose, who was born at Active Pass in the 1770s. Around 1800 he was captured during battle and transported across the old trading route that led through the mountain heart of Vancouver Island into the Clayoquot, where he was sold to Chief Wickaninnish.

A decade later he saw a three-masted schooner drop anchor in the bay. He wasn't allowed to go out to the ship because he was a slave, so he watched the fireworks from Echachist. On the first day, a black-bearded man on board insulted the chief. Next morning the Clayoquots returned in canoes and swarmed up the side of the vessel. Cries carried across the water, and four men climbed the rigging and hid among the crosstrees. Then came smoke and gunfire, and the braves fled.

Next morning the four men were gone from the rigging. A lone figure appeared on deck waving a blanket. The warriors clambered back aboard, bent on plunder. Suddenly there was an ear-shattering explosion. Bodies were hurled hundreds of feet into the air, and shards of wood and iron rained down into the bay for half a mile around. More than two hundred braves died in the final sortie, and many more women and children in the canoes alongside.

Ten-ta-coose was later ransomed to the Hudson's Bay Company for ten blankets. He lived until he was almost a hundred, then his canoe capsized near Fort Langley and he drowned. Young Allard never twigged that he was hearing about the *Tonquin*. As an old man he told a writer called Pinkey McKelvie, who had read *Astoria* and made the connection.

Making connections was an art that had fallen out of vogue in the city, because it meant keeping an eye on the big picture, and the city picture was too damn big. But the connections were there. One night I walked past the Moka House and saw Annie MacLeod inside. She was the great-grandniece of old Joe MacLeod, the earliest skipper of the *Loch Ryan*. I asked her if she knew where Joe got the boat. She had no idea, but she gave me the number of his widow, June MacLeod, who still lived up at Qualicum Beach. June gave me another number, and so on, and so on, until I had made contact with half the Clayoquot old guard.

Len Clay, who got his glasses mixed up with Sam Eadie's on the morning the *Daisy* foundered, lived up on Cedar Hill. He figured he had tracked down the *Norcap*'s skipper in an ancient fish boat registry he had saved since the forties. I cycled over to his house. The registry was wrinkled and yellow as the back of an old fisherman's hand. Len ran his finger down a list to the name Pedersen, and my heart leaped. That was certainly Scandinavian. But his boat had been called *Northcamp*. So close.

Bob Wingen was still kicking, eighty years old and hard at work every day in his new machine shop outside Steveston. I cycled to the ferries and along River Road to his place. He was just about to fly up the coast to troubleshoot an old piece of machinery. Such jaunts were common for him because there were a lot of aging machines on the coast that only he really understood. We talked for hours about the *Tahsis Princess* and his dad and granddad, but not even Bob recalled the origin of the *Norcap*. Finally I got the number of an old fisherman called Charlie Madden, who remembered the *Norcap*, but not the skipper's name. "Ach! It's on the tip of my tongue. I must be getting old."

Next day he phoned back. "Doug Lind. He was a bit of a loner. He ran a fish packing dock up in Quatsino Sound." It turned out my boat came from Winter Harbour, the westernmost settlement in Canada. I had followed the river to its source. Nothing lay beyond Winter Harbour but the open horizon. Next stop: Japan.

AS NEW MACDONALD'S "WANNA MAKE A MOVIE" deadline loomed, everyone polished up their scripts. I bandied a few ideas with Michael Giampa, but I couldn't seem to buckle down and turn one into a screenplay. One night in February it snowed, so I walked down to the Village. Outside the Moka House a guy in an Elmer Fudd hat tried to sell me a watch for six bucks. "It don't work," he said. "But, hey — six bucks!" Other customers shied away, but to me he was kin, a member of the Tribe of Verb, trapped in the moment. His only crime was that he didn't want his head mitred, dovetailed and glued into the gigantic noun we call the Grid. I knew how he felt.

I bought a cappuccino and watched snowflakes swirl between the naked chestnut trees. The deadline was in two weeks. I should be at my desk, writing. But the evening seemed enchanted. Pic-A-Flic's marquee sang to me like a siren. An hour later I headed home through the snow with an old Kurosawa movie called *Rashomon*.

It was a Japanese tale of murder and rape told from four different points of view. It brought to mind the conflicting versions of the *Tonquin* saga. Suddenly that mental flash lit up my frontal lobes and I saw it all: I would write a murder mystery that told the terrible tale of Shannon and Nashon from four different points of view. A redskin/redneck *Fargo* set on the beach near Tofino. Five actors, no sets, all natural lighting.

There was no time to write a script. I scribbled a ten-page outline and made it down to New MacDonald's at five to five on deadline day. I had to borrow a stapler to seal the envelope and a pen to write my name on the outside. By the time I was done, the folks at the front desk were giggling. I was mortified. Why couldn't I be more professional, like the 850 other writers whose submissions filled a small room near the front door?

The front door rattled. It was Michael Giampa, five minutes late, with his outline in hand. We laughed and laughed. Our outlines ended up on the top of the heap. Usually that's a figure of speech, but in this case it was a concrete fact. Naturally we were suspicious when both our movie outlines were chosen out of those 850. What are the chances? I told Michael, "Either they just grabbed the top two, or writing and deadlines don't mix."

Suspicions aside, I was stoked, because New MacDonald's was helmed by Toronto's televisionary, Moses Znaimer — the genius behind Pasheabel's favourite channel Much-Music. People said he was a monomaniac, but I figured his arrogance was honestly come by. New MacDonald's brought me into their tsunami-proof boardroom to meet with Tom, their script editor, who had worked for a summer on a flensing deck up in Whaletown, so he knew the coast. Tom was keen. After the meeting he pumped my hand and said that together we would turn my outline into a great screenplay. I nodded and smiled, but I felt way out of my depth. A million-dollar project seemed roughly on a par with painting a hundred Floatels. And here I was at the wheel.

The Plan: jury-rig a functional script from the wealth of tales I had encountered during my fifteen years in the Clayoquot. I opened with a tale from the Tofino laundromat. The place stayed open all night so that fishermen who got back from a trip at three in the morning could wash their work clothes, and this had made it privy to town's dark side.

One morning the machines were found lying on their sides in an inch of soapy water. The night's mischief had been caught on the security video, a single steady shot of the rows of washers and dryers, with the action unfolding at high speed, to highly comic effect.

At first the laundromat was deserted, with headlights whizzing past outside as the daylight faded. After dark, Jake from the *Oldfield* crew showed up with six garbage bags of laundry. Around midnight Turtle came in with a bottle of scotch, which he plonked down between them on the little table at the front, and its level dropped at frightening rate as they talked and gestured in rapid motion. At 1 AM the pub disgorged a murder of herring fishermen, who were staggering past the window when Turtle waved them inside. Suddenly there were thirty drunks dancing wildly between the rows of machines. Then the number dwindled to ten, then five, then two: a big woman who stumbled blotto between the washers and dryers with her shirt undone, trying to evade the drunken paws of a man half her size, who had stripped down to his ball cap and underpants. At last the woman gave up and lay across the dryers, and they went at it like livestock. Then the laundromat was deserted once more, early traffic whizzed past outside, and the sun came up. The underbelly of small town BC exposed in three minutes flat. A perfect opening to a dark and twisted tale from the coast.

Instead of a hero I created a goat based on the ever-changing New Cop, a youthful Fisheries officer who has just returned to the town where he grew up. The fallout from the laundromat bacchanal leads this young fish cop into the middle of a crab war, like the one between Dick and Jamie. When he tries to enforce peace between the crabbers he discovers the war was sparked by a crazy kid who lost his mind in a diving accident, and now lives out in the wilderness and keeps coming into town to wreak havoc, like Nashon. When the fish cop confronts the crazy kid he finds the body of a beloved old nun from the school, who has just been murdered. Then the murder is recounted from four different points of view, like in Kurosawa's *Rashomon*.

I had the chunks of plot in place, but there was no life in the story, like I couldn't find the ignition key. Then one night I dreamed I was in a little fishing village. Everyone was asleep in rows under the old library. A cat came creeping through the sleeping bodies. I sat up in front of it and said, "Grendel!" and it jumped right inside me. I ran to the north corner of the building and screamed into the night, and the cat came out with the scream and went howling away through the dark trees.

I thought I woke screaming, but the scream was just a dry croak. What the hell was that about? I knew Grendel was a character in *Beowulf*, that epic Norse poem which you're supposed to read in college. My prof said it was the genesis of western literature, but I never got around to reading it, what with all the drinking. I figured now might be a good time to start, even though it was three in the morning.

I fired up the computer and stared into the screen, dimly aware that around the world a legion of kindred souls cowled over their solitary panes of light, entranced by these stained-glass windows that opened on the collective unconscious. I found *Beowulf* in the ghostly stacks of a library somewhere in Cyberia, and read it with growing wonder: Beowulf, a youthful warrior, returns to the town where he grew up to find the place terrorized by Grendel, a monster who lives out in the wilderness and keeps coming into town to wreak havoc. Beowulf deals with Grendel, then he has to deal with Grendel's mother. Somehow, without even reading it, I had ripped off *Beowulf.*

In a flash I had the key to my screenplay: the old nun. She was Grendel's mother. After the fish cop dealt with the crazy kid he had to deal with the old nun, a monster who had been left in charge of town's children for years, and had psychically devoured them one by one, a creature so terrible she could only be glimpsed sidelong between the other characters' conflicting accounts.

New MacDonald's loved the screenplay, and shook money from their sides like a big wet dog shakes rain. They told me to get cracking on the second draft, and sent reams of notes written by all sorts of people I hadn't even met. One note said I should cut the helicopter scenes for budgetary reasons. Another said I should add more helicopter scenes to boost production value. My head told me I had to find some way to incorporate these notes, but my heart told me to ignore them. Since that Beowulf dream, the human soul seemed like a fathomless mystery with the conscious mind bobbing on top. What angel tells the fisherman where to cast his net?

I filed the second draft in late October. Months passed, and still no word. Around Christmas Shamess Shute called to say he'd landed the gig of Assistant Director on my movie. I said that couldn't be, I hadn't finished writing it yet. Awkward moment. When I e-mailed New MacDonald's they said that Tom, the script editor, had taken my screenplay and run with it. I thought they were speaking figuratively until they mailed me the final draft. Tom's version read like a parody of mine. The characters walked around saying things that were the opposite of all I held sacred, the evil nun had been changed into a guy so that the part could be played by Charles from M*A*S*H, and not one of my small town tales remained. My dark vision had been rendered generic as a Happy Meal.

When Moses came down from Toronto to oversee the shoot I phoned him up and said his WANNA MAKE A MOVIE? e-mail should really have said WANNA MAKE A SAUSAGE? He said he could explain and invited me over to his suite, a whole turret of the Empress Hotel, with a killer view of the parliament buildings. Rumour said Moses worked 24/7, so I was not surprised to see reams of screenplays piled around the big four-poster bed, and miles of telephone lines snaking across the hardwood floor. But I *was* surprised when Moses stepped out of the en suite wearing nothing but a toothy grin and handed me a bamboo cane. He confessed that what he'd done to my movie was "just plain wrong", and I would be well within my rights to thrash him like a schoolgirl.

"Fair enough," I said, and swished the bamboo through the air to test its spring, while Moses hopped from foot to foot in front of the four-poster, whimpering with anticipation.

Okay, that never happened. It's another yarn, like the Tale of Mordecai, although everything that lies between those two tales is pretty much as I remember it. In fact, shortly after I signed on with New MacDonald's, Moses left for the greener pastures of Alberta, where he had purchased an educational television network. His singular vision was replaced by a committee, whose master plan was to set up shop in Vancouver. But the Feds wouldn't give them a broadcast license. The only toehold on the west coast was Vancouver Island, so to get that license they promised to put millions into local film production. The following year a Vancouver license came up for bids, New MacDonald's nabbed it, and the Island station became a white elephant. When it came time to shoot my film they hired a production company from Vancouver, which for some reason the Feds still counted as local film production, and the Island's film community was leery about blowing the whistle on the scam in case they burned their bridges with the corporation.

But to me, corporations are not to be feared. They're simply a kind of engine that generates cash, and I learned on the *Loch Ryan* that it's important not to let the engine get on top of you. Writers routinely come to grief by mistaking entities like New MacDonald's for something human, then start screaming when it eats their baby. Fortunately, I sold them Kurosawa's baby.

And that's the story of how I lost my first feature film. It was a setback, but no worse than when Joe MacLeod ran the *Muns* aground at Hesquiat, and nowhere near as bad as the time Sam Eadie lost the *Daisy*, five miles out on a lonely sea. At least I still had my computer. My first few seasons writing in the city felt like a great success, like the sort of herring opening fishermen talk about for years to come. I missed Tough City when I thought about it, but mostly I thought about what lay ahead. In the offing, the vast expanse of the human soul shone like a new ocean. I wanted to explore its shores, salvage stories from the shipwreck of my life and turn them into something new, like young Tom Wingen, when he came through the Graveyard and found the Clayoquot, green and full of dreams waiting to be shaken awake.

Epilogue

WHEN SPRING CAME I RENTED A GRAND AM AND blasted up to Clayoquot to shoot test footage for my glass float film. Town seemed different. Conehead and Barry Grumbach had drunk themselves to death, there was a giant hotel on the site of Henry's A-frame, Campbell Street was done up like an orca red light district, and Gwen and Pasheabel's house was gone. Gwen had passed the place on to an artist called Jan, and one morning *über*-developer Chris Lefevre showed up at her door and shook her hand. "I have a disease," he said. "I can't stop buying land in Tofino."

It's a socially acceptable disease. He tore Gwen's house out of the waterfront like an old kidney and put up a condo. His insurance company checked the last big cedar, which towered over the property, and decided it had to come down because it was rotten inside. When the chainsaw crew arrived a young Québecois who had set up shop in the remains of my pyramid climbed into the candelabra and won a reprieve. A campaign sprung up to save the tree. Chris sensed a sea-change and pledged $25,000 to the cause. The whole town kicked in, Fredy built a massive metal frame around the giant cedar, and the result was hideous, like Gaia in a polio brace. Chris never came through with the coin he promised, and Ralph Tieleman had started a

"Free The Tree" campaign.

Ralph had quit painting and now ran a surf shop on the hill above the pub. He was hosing sand off the rental boards when I drove past. I yelled, "Hey, hoser!" He didn't even look round, so I went inside and rented a wetsuit for the film shoot. For the first five minutes he ignored me and pretended to flip through some files. Then he made me fill out a draconian rental form. Then when I tried to pay he waved my card away. "That's okay, Andrew." Ralph hadn't changed at all. What a relief.

It turned out Tough City's corporate makeover was largely cosmetic. Henry's A-frame was gone, but Henry remained. He had moved into the loft of his carving shed fifty feet down the beach, with the same view and the same pile of tools, and when I dropped in to visit he seemed much more concerned about a bad cramp in his leg than about the giant hotel next door. Chris from the *Oldfield* was selling fish and chips out of a tin shed across from Chestermans Beach, surfer Adam had started an Internet café next to it, Crabber Dave had given up on the city and bought a condo where the giant hollow cedar once stood, and Al Anderson had been elected major.

Out on Strawberry Island, Rod sat in his wheelhouse under his curved wall of books, the mysterious anchor from Templar Channel lashed to the dock outside. After ignoring him for a year, the government scientists down in the city saw an article about the anchor in the *New York Times*. The following week they landed on the dock in a helicopter and ran around waving clipboards and pens and warning Rod to disband his Indiana Jones school of archeology. "They want everything fitted into their damn pigeonholes," he said.

Behind Strawberry Island, the *Loch Ryan* was moored at Peter's private dock, which he had salvaged from a logging camp up in Bedwell Sound. The engine started first crank. She was a good old boat. I chugged along the harbourfront, rounded Grice Point into Father Charles Channel and ran her towards the open horizon. Next stop: Japan. Usually that's a figure of speech, but in this case it was a fact. The National Film Board was sending Pasheabel and me to Japan to scout locations for my glass float movie. Next week we would fly to Tokyo, drive down the coast, and search for a little fishing village like Tofino, the sort where, fifty years ago, local glassblowers made those glass floats from smashed-up sake bottles. What a strange new world. I was in league with the Feds.

On shore the sky had been overcast, but out on the water the gloom broke into silver patches, and jagged islands shone through the mist in a dozen shades of gray. The channel looked like the entrance to Valhalla.

I love this ragged coast. Long after the rest of the world had hardened into nouns, this place remained a bright, soft verb. Now a great tide was sweeping us from adventure into capital, and as Fred Tibbs knows, you can only buck the tide till your arms get tired.

But nouns, verbs — those are just words. What is real is the wood of the *Loch Ryan*'s wheel creaking under my palm, the salt air blowing in my face through the wheelhouse window, and the changes I felt in my soul as the mystery and machinery of this good old boat carried me back to the city from the Clayoquot, and the magical forest of my youth.

Acknowledgments

Written histories lifted from Walter Guppy's *Eighty Years in Tofino* and *Clayoquot Soundings*, Bob Bossin's *Settling Clayoquot*, and G. M. Sproat's *Scenes and Studies of Savage Life*. Shipwreck tales pirated from T. W. Paterson's *British Columbia Shipwrecks* and *Shipwrecks of British Columbia* by Fred Rogers. Nuu-chah-nulth lore gleaned from *Teachings of the Tides* by David Ellis and Luke Swan, *The West Coast People* by E. Y. Arima, *Nuu-Chah-Nulth Voices*, and the extensive works of Phillip Drucker. Oral histories supplied by Whitey Bernard, Henry Nola, Bob Wingen, Neil Botting, Len Clay, Joe Martin, Rod Palm, Ken Gibson and Barry Grumbach.

Audrey McClellan edited *The Last Voyage of the Loch Ryan* for New Star Books. Frank Harper, Kevin Gillese, Peter Campbell, Sid Tafler, Carol Toller, Ross Crockford and Rolf Maurer also read and commented on the manuscript in its various stages.

Special thanks to my daughter Pasheabel, without whose safe anchorage I might be living in a bus station somewhere; and to the Canada Council for the Arts, for ponying up a pile of cash just when I needed it most.

Victoria
July 1, 2004

ΠΚ
DICK (HOP SCOTCH)